The Limits of Masculinity

ANDREW TOLSON

TAVISTOCK PUBLICATIONS

First published in 1977 by
Tavistock Publications Limited
11 New Fetter Lane,
London EC4P 4EE
Printed in Great Britain by
Richard Clay (The Chaucer
Press) Ltd, Bungay, Suffolk

© Andrew Tolson 1977

ISBN 0 422 75930 9 (hardbound)
ISBN 0 422 75940 6 (paperback)

Contents

1

God's gift to women?

'According to usage and conventions which are at last being questioned but have by no means been overcome, the social presence of a woman is different in kind from that of a man. A man's presence is dependent upon the promise of power which he embodies. If the promise is large and credible his presence is striking. If it is small or incredible, he is found to have little presence ... A man's presence suggests what he is capable of doing to you or for you. His presence may be fabricated, in the sense that he pretends to be capable of what he is not. But the pretence is always towards a power which he exercises on others.'

(John Berger, 1972a : 45–6)

For most people, women as well as men, 'masculinity' is a taken for granted part of everyday life. There is a masculine aura of competence, a way of talking and behaving towards others, which is immediately recognized. In part, images of masculinity enter into our most intimate communications – they are enshrined in social rituals and customs. We can recall a whole repertoire of popular phrases and aphorisms – 'take it like a

7

man'; 'big boys don't cry' – by which we continue to define personal experience. But also, to some extent, masculinity is institutionalized. It is part of a formal language, or 'code', built into the framework of social organization. There are men's jobs, men's recreations, men's social groups – a sexual division of labour based on the most fundamental of all assumptions, that 'a woman's place is in the home'.

It is because we share these expectations of masculinity that we are able to respond to John Berger's description of a man's social presence. The 'promise of power' is at the centre of a network of conventional masculine characteristics: authority, self-assertion, competitiveness, aggression, physical strength. And Berger's way of putting it is particularly suggestive, for he shows how 'presence' – a certain style of behaviour, an outward presentation – becomes part of an internal self-image. In his social life a man will cultivate, and even fabricate, his masculine presence. In his fantasies he will pursue sexual scenarios of seduction and possession. And in his most intense emotional experience it is the mystery of a woman's presence that stimulates his desire:

> 'It was with a woman's presence that man fell in love. That part of a man which was submissive was mesmerized with the attention which she bestowed upon herself, and he dreamt of her bestowing the same attention upon himself ... That part of a man which was masterful dreamt of possessing, not her body – this he called lust – but the variable mystery of her presence.'

> (John Berger, 1972b : 151)

Thus, masculinity comprises a structure of inter-related conventions. In this book I shall try to unravel this structure, looking for typical patterns and their social foundations. I shall look at both sides of the masculine presence – the outward show, and the psychic drama – and I shall try to trace connections, and contradictions, between these two spheres. I shall also analyse some of the boundaries of 'social presence' – exploring the *limits* of masculinity. As Berger himself points out, the rituals of masculine behaviour are increasingly under attack. Despite its apparent permanence, and behind the evocation of sexual recognition, the masculine character is becoming highly volatile, and insecure.

In Birmingham, in January 1973, an unusual advertisement appeared in the local Women's Liberation Newsletter:

MEN'S LIBERATION

'In a recent conversation with a woman in Women's Liberation, she made an observation about the wry laughter which greets any comment of the type, "But my man is liberated!" The wry quality of the laughter is worth looking at. It comes from a dual recognition in the form of, "Yes, I suppose that's what I sometimes think," and, "But it's not true, he's not really liberated." The recognition that, if Women's Liberation has been created by women as a possibility within our society; men's liberation hasn't even got started.

The many husbands and boyfriends, liberals and leftwingers who are "sympathetic" to Women's Liberation don't know, are not interested, won't acknowledge this fact. But women know the extent of men's liberation ... They know from their collective experience of countless put-downs by men, and the many times they have been invited to prop up the male ego, or give the gratifying reflection.

'These are some of the ways in which male security rests upon female repression. And to the extent that this is the case, it is hard to see why men should desire liberation. But there is another side to the coin. For what a sexist society makes of the male role is an image of maleness, of masculinity, which is frequently as limiting to the man as the image of femininity is to the woman. The possibility of men's liberation then, rests upon an awareness by men of the limitations imposed upon them by a sexist society ...'

Men's liberation? My own attention to this advert was directed by a friend, and without her persuasion I do not think I would have taken it very seriously. What are these 'limitations' of masculinity? Isn't 'sexism' a woman's problem? It was under a fair amount of pressure, and certainly not with any spontaneous enlightenment, that I found myself attending the first meeting of a proposed 'men's group'.

9

It is important I think, straight away, to sketch some of the background to that first meeting. Like four others, out of the seven who came, I lived in close contact with the academic world. I had studied at the university since 1968, and so had lived through what came to be known as the 'student movement', which culminated in the late 'sixties in a series of strikes and sit-ins. The student movement had close connections with a youthful, middle-class 'counter-culture' – an extension of the pop/hippy/drug scene of previous years. By the beginning of the 'seventies, every major city had its 'alternative society': a network of small, semi-political groups (encounter groups, community activists, 'underground' publications, collective houses, and communes) which formed a kind of infrastructure to so-called 'straight' society. But at the turn of the decade, this 'alternative' world was confronted – and in its male-chauvinist aspects, decisively criticized – by the advent of feminism. By 1973, no man with my kind of background could avoid a direct encounter with Women's Liberation.

For many liberal middle-class men, the growth of a feminist consciousness represented a challenge. At the time our group was formed we sensed a collective spirit among the women we knew. It seemed that their lives were opening out – into new groups, experimental relationships, and forms of political action. Their solidarity was carried over into family life, demanding a constructive attitude from men to women's independence. As men, we felt trapped in our own exclusion – not because we were excluded from women's activities, but because we had no equivalent 'liberation' for ourselves. Together, we would fall into the conventional 'matiness' of the pub, a mutual back-slapping, designed to repress as much as it expresses. It was impossible to talk to other men about personal feelings of weakness or jealousy. A masculine 'mask of silence' concealed the emptiness of our emotional lives.

In many ways, it was a good thing that we were able to share the middle-class cultural world, for that at first was all we had in common. Our first meetings were charged with a reticence we could not comprehend. We had vague notions of coming to terms with the feminist critique of masculinity, and maybe acting as 'auxiliaries' to the Women's Movement.

We wanted to rediscover the experience of becoming a man – taking seriously our shortcomings, and learning from the analysis. But we soon discovered that no one really knew, or could express, why he had joined the men's group in the first place. As men, we had no language to formulate our uncertainties; no way of showing to others our responsiveness or concern. As radical, intellectual, liberal middle-class men, with everything seemingly in our favour – we could not understand the impact of feminism on our lives.

It is our first, tentative, step beyond the mask of silence that has formed the perspective of this book. Out of the defensiveness that dominated our first meetings, we began to discover new forms of self-expression, and new ways of relating to each other. We began to analyse our own experience, not only in the light of feminist theory, but also through our own preoccupations. I do not want to make great claims for this – other men's groups have developed their own projects and perspectives. But it is important for me to emphasize that the basis of this book is a particular experience – incomplete, perhaps one-sided, but a start. I have tried to fill out the historical context; to analyse the way masculinity colours everyday life; and to trace through some aspects of men's consciousness, in the context of the small men's group. Readers, who so wish, may read the final chapter first – where on the basis of the Birmingham experience, processes of 'consciousness-raising' and questions of 'sexual politics' are discussed in greater detail.

The form of this book consists of three basic arguments which, as they constitute the framework of my analysis, I will summarize in advance. Together these arguments make up what I take to be the essence of the feminist understanding of sexuality – in its cultural, historical, and political contexts. Part of the significance of this understanding, and part of the influence of the Women's Movement, arises from its critique of the immediate situation of women, and its development of a theory of sexuality and society in its wider implications. This theory includes a feminist analysis of masculinity, which it is possible for men themselves to comprehend.

My starting point is perhaps the most basic of all feminist

propositions: the distinction between biology and culture. When we talk about 'masculinity', or when we respond to the masculine 'social presence', we draw upon certain specific forms of social knowledge. This is to say, although certain aspects of sexual behaviour are obviously functions of biological *sex* (including genetic aptitude and physical development), by far the major part of sexuality is *cultural* (encompassing personality, social behaviour; and involving symbolic meanings transmitted in linguistic communication). This argument is put most clearly by Ann Oakley, in her book, *Sex, Gender and Society*. There is 'sex', the biological difference, and there is 'gender', or 'gender identity' – the cultural significance attached to sexuality:

> ' "Sex" is a biological term: "gender" a psychological and cultural one. Common sense suggests that they are merely two ways of looking at the same division and that someone who belongs to, say, the female sex will automatically belong to the corresponding (feminine) gender. In reality this is not so. To be a man or a woman, a boy or a girl, is as much a function of dress, gesture, occupation, social network and personality, as it is of possessing a particular set of genitals.[1]
>
> (Ann Oakley, 1972:158)

This definition of 'gender' is important, because it allows us to appreciate the highly particular ways in which 'masculinity' is commonly understood. We can begin to acknowledge that 'masculinity' is not simply the opposite of 'femininity', but that there are many types of gender identity (including homosexual and trans-sexual identities), and different expressions of masculinity within and between different cultures. The characteristics we define as 'masculine' are culture-specific: every aspect of our 'masculine presence' is contradicted in other cultures and societies. In our society masculinity is the dominant, prestigious form of gender identity – but again, this is not necessarily so in other social formations.

In Western, industrialized, capitalist societies, definitions of masculinity are bound up with definitions of work. Whether it is in terms of physical strength or mechanical expertise, or in terms of ambition and competitiveness, the qualities needed by the successful worker are closely related to those of the successful man. As individuals, men are brought up to value work, as an end in itself, and to fix their personal identities around particular occupations. The roots of gender identity are interfused with expectations of achievement – 'becoming someone' through working, 'making something of yourself'. It is this personal identity that insists on 'the right to work', to be a breadwinner for the family, and which is threatened by lay-off or redundancy. There is in our society a collective masculine culture of work that makes firm distinctions between 'work' and 'non-work', 'work' and 'leisure', or 'career' and 'family'. It is a characteristic of such dichotomies that 'non-work' is not seen as a complement to 'work', but as its antithesis – as compensation for effort, or reward for success. As he moves between the demarcated spheres of his existence, a man must negotiate barriers of definition and find ways of coping with the shifting of his identity.

In the course of this book I shall explore some of the social limitations of masculinity. In particular I shall emphasize the ways in which gender identities, as they are presently defined, obscure social possibilities for men themselves. In their working lives many men are condemned to a quest for personal rewards which they cannot hope to realize. Bound to a hier-archical ladder of achievement, they are doomed to follow a mirage of success, an ever-retreating image of having 'made it'. At home, with their insistence on status, they are prevented from enjoying certain kinds of domestic labour ('housework') and childcare. Social prestige becomes a psychological barrier, limiting their potentiality for personal relationships.

Thus, masculinity is a culturally specific and socially functional 'gender identity', with peculiar (often negative) consequences for men themselves. This, the first feminist proposition, leads to a second: that if gender is cultural and social, then it is also *historical* – sexuality is not the same for different generations. There is no 'universal' masculinity, but rather a varying masculine experience of each succeeding social epoch. The feminist-historical perspective points to the discontinuous nature of personal life, and feminist historians have begun to study the 'hidden' history, not only of women, but also of the organization of domesticity, the family, and the sexual division of labour:

'Capitalism brought new relationships of property and domination. It brought into being a class which did not own the means of production, "free" labourers who had to sell their labour power on the market. It started to dissolve all previous forms of ownership. But men still owned their women body and soul long after they themselves ceased to be the property of other men. Men continued to own and control female creative capacity in the family and to assume that the subordination of women in society was just and natural – though the consequences of this for women from different classes were not the same. Patriarchy, the power of men as a sex to dispose of women's capacity to labour, especially in the family, has not had a direct and simple relationship to class exploitation.'

(Sheila Rowbotham, 1973a :ix)

In part, this history of sexuality is a history of the 'origins' of gender identity. The history of masculinity is often remembered with nostalgia – notions of paternal inheritance, memories of collective solidarity, and hard, physical toil. It is important to a man that he can talk about his ancestors, his property, his work – and that he can project himself into the past. He can appeal to history for confirmation of his birthright. He can invoke the ancient law of 'patriarchy': the continuing symbolic power associated with property inheritance, the organization of the family, and the maintenance of male supremacy. This history is truly 'hidden', not only because it is largely unexamined by historians, but also because it enters the present unconsciously – in cultural predispositions beneath the surface of individual awareness. In a capitalist age of corporate property, where the productive functions of the family have declined, patriarchy is a powerful anachronism. It provides a man with a reference point for self-justification; and it still broods on, like a recurring dream, in the masculine gender identity.

But the feminist-historical perspective also has its focus fixed on contemporary society. The starting point for the

14

account of patriarchy is a new experience of sexual insecurity; and I shall look, in later chapters, at some dimensions of this experience – for it is the immediate 'conjuncture', of the feminist critique. On one level, certain phenomena of the post-war consumer society (the growth of advertising, fashion, pop-culture, TV) have both reflected and glamorized a 'fragmentation' of gender-identities – a confusing, shifting definition of 'masculine' and 'feminine'. 'Unisex' appeared, in the 'sixties, as its public facade; but at the same time it glossed over a number of more problematic sexual experiences – witnessed by the so-called 'generation gap', and by conflicting attitudes to 'permissiveness' and 'the pill'. At a deeper level it appears that these experiences of the 'sixties were part of a historical transformation in the organization of personal life. The 'consumer society' brought to final fruition a long-term tendency of industrial capitalism to divide 'work' and 'home', and to create a proletariat for which 'leisure' (home-centred family relationships) is the reward for alienated labour:

> 'Peasants and other pre-capitalist labourers were governed by the same social relations "inside" and "outside" work; the proletarian, by contrast, was a "free" man or woman outside work. By splitting society between "work" and "life", proletarianization created the conditions under which men and women looked to themselves, outside the division of labour, for meaning and purpose ... Proletarianization generated new needs – for trust, intimacy and self-knowledge, for example – which intensified the weight of meaning attached to the personal relations of the family. The organization of production around alienated labour encouraged the creation of a separate sphere of life in which personal relations were pursued as ends in themselves.'

> (Eli Zaretsky, 1976:65–6)

For all men, particularly within certain fractions of the middle class, the post-war experience has been disturbing. There is a contemporary 'problem of masculinity', involving an adjustment to disintegrating images of 'self'. This is a difficult problem to specify, because in public debate it is clouded by 'commonsense', and is unacknowledged by many men themselves. It is apparent that in so far as our society remains patriarchal, it works for the benefit of men – in employment, civil law, and informal relationships. Straight men are not 'oppressed' by patriarchy in the same ways as women or gays. Equally, many aspects of industrial capitalism, and the development of what Zaretsky calls 'proletarianization', have simply accentuated tendencies of masculine culture. In the consumer society, ideas of 'affluence', 'leisure', and the split between 'work' and 'home' are masculine ideas – there is no such split for the 'housewife'. But despite the institutionalization of male supremacy, and behind the masculine social presence, individual men are beginning to lose some of their self-confidence. Partly, the sheer complexity of the modern state sets firm limits on personal authority. Even at 'the top' a successful careerist cannot simply rule by personal charisma or domination. And partly, the sexual tensions of the 'sixties, effects of the 'permissive society', have undermined the masculine 'presence'. In a consumer society, sexuality is publicized, criticized, compared. It is not so easy for men to maintain the pretence of sexual bravado.

Several feminist writers have commented on this 'problem of masculinity' – the defensive insecurity of men in post-war society. What is at stake, is the maintenance, by an individual man, of his patriarchal privilege, in a context where it is progressively undermined. Middle-class men, especially, find their expectations contradicted – by bureaucracy at work, or by the failure of real sexuality to live up to its consumer image. Some men have turned in on themselves, to withdrawal and introspection, or to the obsessive pursuit of 'hobbies'. At the heart of the masculine experience they have discovered a sense of futility. And women have observed the shallowness of the masculine 'presence', as men have tried to conceal their personal uncertainties:

'If men were really men, I thought, then they would be willing to take responsibility for their actions and reactions. They would be willing to confront themselves as people instead of as godlike images. They would be able to look at a woman on the street with a clear, wholesome expression, sexually appreciative but not predatory ... I considered *anything* valid that was an expression of genuine feeling, an expression of honest experience. But there, precisely, was where men failed. Because they would rather do anything, than admit to what they genuinely feel ... would rather flatter, seduce, cajole, or humour a woman than admit to hostility and its ever-present companion, fear.'

(Ingrid Bengis, 1973:41–4)

As women have explored the social and historical roots of their own oppression, one of their demands has been for men to do the same:

'At the same time I sensed something very complicated going on in the heads of men who were about my age. It's for them to write about this. I wish they would very soon. The most eloquent records exist in the songs we've been listening to since the sixties ... their songs are really often very scared. It's as if they sense a threat to the old way of being a man, before women's liberation became a movement. Part of them wants really to crush the new ways in which women behave, both in bed and outside, but the other part of them goes out to women because they are against how most men put them down.'

(Sheila Rowbotham, 1973b:21–2)

It is at this point in the feminist argument, that a third basic proposition is introduced: the development of 'sexual politics'. For the analysis of sexuality in its cultural and historical aspects bring into focus its *political* significance, in relationships of power and conflict. There is a 'politics of sexuality', not only because of the use of sex-defined categories by politicians (the notion of the 'housewife' in rhetoric about rising prices), but also because sexual relationships are *power* relationships, which work to the detriment of women. Definitions of gender enter into some of the basic meanings attached to work, leisure, family life. So all political struggles to transform the social organization of experience are bound to confront sexual prejudice and discrimination.

For men, the major significance of feminist politics has been its attempt to extend the arena of political debate, to encompass the politics of personal life. The most radical innovation of feminism has been its insistence that 'the personal is political' – that personal experience, as well as theories and tactics, are to be included in the transformation of social relationships. Women have recognized that their oppression touches on the most intimate and unconscious areas of experience – aspects of fantasy, imagination, and personality. At the centre of the struggle are questions of language and symbolism in everyday communication. Women's politics are necessarily *cultural politics* – directed at sexual stereotypes, and commonsense definitions of 'femininity'.

As a first step towards the transformation of gender identity, the Women's Liberation Movement has pioneered the activity of 'consciousness-raising' – the formation of small, local, informal groups, to overcome barriers of personal silence and to support individuals' attempts to break daily routines. As Ingrid Bengis puts it: 'Ultimately, it is precisely our willingness to experiment with our own lives that has made us a marked generation' (1973:53).

This feminist insistence on 'consciousness-raising' issues a powerful challenge to men. In the first place it undermines the masculine definition of 'politics' as such. Most male-dominated political groups prefer to ignore problems of 'personalities'; following the traditional masculine practice, they preserve the 'home' as a cocoon of emotional retreat. Even the tired revolutionary comes home to his 'wife and kids'. More fundamentally – and this was the rationale for our men's group – feminism explicitly invites men themselves to change, to discover new forms of masculine identity. It is a long and difficult process: men are often unable to talk about themselves, or to explore their relationships with others. In their personal lives men are usually dogmatic, aggressively conservative. But the experience of gender-fragmentation, and the uncertainties of 'proletarianization', are forcing more and more men into positions of psychological stress. Here the example and the challenge of Women's Liberation opens up possibilities for the future:

'Men ... are ashamed of their own sensitivity to suffering and love because they have been taught to regard these as feminine. They are afraid of becoming feminine because this means that other men will despise them, we will despise them and they will despise themselves. Men are as afraid of being rejected and despised as we are. They have only a defensive solidarity ... We are moving towards a new world together but development is an uneven and painful process. We must be honest and help one another until they find a new way to express and organize themselves towards us. The generalization of our consciousness of our own subordination enables them to discover a new manner of being men.'

(Sheila Rowbotham, 1973b:43)

What is this 'new manner of being men'? How is it discovered? I think it is important to recognize that men's 'consciousness-raising has not, and cannot, follow a path identical to Women's Liberation. Because masculinity is the dominant form of gender identity, there can be no question of men vicariously sharing the excitement of self-expression and discovery which women have achieved. There are limitations to the ways men can organize – ambiguities inherent in the very notion of 'men's politics', which the embryonic 'men's movement' has discovered. On the personal level, I think we must also recognize that many men remain distanced from their own emotions. Whereas feminist women are able to theorize *from* their own experience, preserving its nuances and sensations, men, even at their most perceptive, seem to theorize *about* themselves, analysing from the outside.

So it is within strictly defined parameters that I am arguing that the 'new manner of being men' is essentially a discovery of possibilities. Out of the experience of post-war society, and in the context of Women's Liberation, it has become possible for men to de-construct their personal lives. Some men have begun to penetrate the mysteries of the masculine presence, and to reject the 'normal' way of being a man. The experience is difficult and most men need to be shocked, or driven, to its threshold. There is a barrier of fear, compounded by tortured postures of ignorance and guilt. But with the critical support of others, in a consciousness-raising group, it is an immediate relief to discuss the experience of sexual anxiety. It is a challenge to discover alternative forms of work, and domestic living. It is equally vital to understand the social implications of masculinity – its prejudice and limited horizons. For socialist men especially, working towards a new society of truly free and equal relationships, consciousness-raising is a necessary social practice:

> 'The popular image of a successful man combines dominance over women, in social relations, and over other men, in the occupational world. But being a master has its burdens. It is not really possible for two persons to have a free relationship when one holds the balance of power over the other ... Persons bent on dominance are inhibited from developing themselves. Part of the price most men must pay for being dominant in one situation is subscribing to a system in which they themselves are subordinated in another situation. The alternative is a system in which men share, among themselves and with women, rather than strive for a dominant role.'
>
> (Jack Sawyer, 1974:171)

In this book I have not only examined feminist arguments about masculinity as a form of gender identity; I have also tried, within the limits of a masculine sensibility, to express something of the lived experience, the mystery, and the burden, of being a man in our society. Where possible I have illustrated my argument with personal accounts, taken from other books or from taped interviews. I have included lengthy extracts from some interviews, to give evidence of varying forms of masculine self-expression.

I have also written about myself, as my own experience of masculinity is relevant. I have written from personal experience about boyhood and about consciousness-raising – experiences of identity formation and change. There remain, of course, many aspects of masculinity which lie outside my own experience – I am young, unmarried, and middle class – and I cannot pretend that my personal impressions are a substitute for systematic analysis. But what, above all, this book is about, is the recognition that without the personal dimension, social theory is meaningless. This recognition is at the heart of the feminist perspective – made necessary by its critical focus on sexuality and consciousness. And it is an inability to make this recognition, that in one respect, defines the limits of masculinity.

2

Boys will be boys

'A father, Stephen said, battling against hopelessness, is a necessary evil.'

(James Joyce, *Ulysses*)

The foundations of masculinity are laid down in boyhood, in a boy's experience of family, school, and his peers. The family provides a basic emotional orientation, which is extended – institutionally in the education system and informally in the cultures of peer-groups – through to adolescence and manhood. In this chapter I shall try to recapture something of the experience of becoming a man; and I shall focus on the ways in which masculinity is *institutionalized*. The family, the school, and the peer-group, together make up the primary context of masculine 'socialization' – in which a boy's emerging sense of himself is directed into socially acceptable behaviour. His taken-for-granted 'masculine presence' is shaped by a systematic process of 'gender-identification'.

To some extent, an insistence upon the institutionalized aspects of boyhood experience goes against the grain of common assumption. In our society we prefer to think of childhood as a period of relative freedom and experimentation. Every childhood is uniquely personal – a particular blend of situation and fantasy. Boyhood experiences are romanticized – as daring exploits, and dramatic confrontations. But right at the heart of these experiences, as the thread of memory and imagination which binds them together, is a growing sense of what it means to be a man. Boyhood is also enveloped by a masculine sensibility – an awareness of the power conferred upon men by the world of work and money. And because of the form in which this masculinity appears, because of the specific ways in which masculine feelings are structured, a boy begins to feel ambivalent about his masculinity, and begins to feel the need to 'prove himself'.

The family

Typical patterns of masculine behaviour are rooted in conventional family relationships. Parents tend to reproduce what they have learned from their parents, enshrined in 'commonsense' formulas – 'big boys don't cry', 'boys will be boys'. Sons (and daughters) follow the precepts of parents, learning by identification and example. Children are, of course, physically dependent on adults – and the family builds upon this material dependence by reinforcing parental *authority* (sanctioned by the threat of withdrawal of care), and reproducing conventions of *sexuality* (against the threat of the child's exclusion from a world of stereotyped sex-roles). In the family the child's physical dependence becomes a psychological dependence. Family life is 'normalized' – it structures the only world a young child knows.

However, within the world of the family, there is an internal emotional development specific to boys. Manhood is a perpetual future, a vision of inheritance, an emptiness waiting to be filled. As a boy there is a sense that one's destiny is somehow bound up with an image of father – his achievement at work, his status in the home. In part, father's 'presence' seems to contain a promise of fulfilment – an affirmation of masculine power – and this feeling is mysterious, generated out of a 'patriarchal bond' between father and son. The anticipated inheritance is partly a sense of becoming what you already are – your father's son – ratified by a common surname. But to a greater extent, a boy's paternal image is related to the specific figure of father in the home. Here, in its mixture of awkwardness and authority, paternal masculinity appears attractive – and yet alien and strangely threatening.

Within the family, masculinity is structured in *ambivalence*. A boy's 'gender-identification' (becoming a man, becoming like his father) is disturbed by his alienation from his father and by his perception of father's absence from the home. Father appears alien, not only because he legislates and punishes (the 'authoritarian' father-figure) but also, more significantly, because his 'masculine presence' can only be construed in his physical *absence* – his distance from family affairs. Father is an outsider because he goes 'out to work'. The brutality of his 'presence' lies not so much in acts of domestic violence (though these cannot be minimized), as in a general masculine estrangement, conditioned by the reality of work. Consequently, as social psychologists are beginning to recognize, the identification of a boy with his father is often problematic:

'... fathers are not at home nearly as much as mothers are. This means that the major psychodynamic process by which sex-roles are learned – the process of identification – is available only minimally to boys since their natural identification objects, their fathers, are simply not around much of the time to serve as models. Illustrative of the children's awareness of this state of affairs, many subjects expressed themselves in the following vein: "My father ... I don't see him very often." "It's harder to know about boys (than about girls) ... Father hardly has time to talk to me." "Men are harder to tell about ... to tell the truth, my father isn't around much."

The absence of fathers means, again that much of male behaviour has to be learned by trial and error and indirection. One outcome of this state of affairs is the fact that boys, as a group, tend to resemble their fathers in personality and attitudes much less than girls resemble their mothers ...

'In addition to the effect of the relative absence of fathers from boys' experience we also have evidence that the relations between boys and their fathers tend to be less good than those between girls and their mothers or fathers ...'

(Ruth E. Hartley, 1974:8)

Obviously it is vital, for the family as a whole, how father's absence is understood; and I shall argue that mother occupies a pivotal role in interpreting his position. But for the moment I want to emphasize the personal outcome of a boy's perception of his father. To the boy, masculinity is both mysterious and attractive (in its promise of a world of work and power) and yet, at the same time, threatening (in its strangeness, and emotional distance). It is, at first, a paradox. It works both ways; attracts and repels in dynamic contradiction. This simultaneous distance and attraction is internalized as a permanent emotional tension that the individual must, in some way, strive to overcome. Self-realization can only be achieved through a confrontation with father's absence; and, by extension, through the emotional uncertainty a boy feels within himself.

A boy's identification with his father is the foundation for all his subsequent experience. As he grows up, the ambivalent structure of his masculine identification becomes a quest for resolution, and a boy develops a compulsive need for recognition and reward. In the culture of masculinity, rewards are always distant, at a premium. They must be fought over, competitively, through a long struggle for supremacy. As I shall indicate, the institutions of school and peer-group are explicitly organized around the principle of struggle: they present to their members a regulated structure of status and achievement. But what the institutional 'rat-race' is designed to conceal, and what remains hidden in the masculine character, is the emotional insecurity, the ambivalent identification, that started the process in the first place.

Looking back, the world of childhood seems a haze of dimly perceived images. I can remember disconnected details: a fire in the downstairs room where I slept when I had measles; bars on the bedroom window to prevent children falling out. I can also, emphatically, sense the presence of my father – with un-familiar smells of beer and tobacco, and a rough, red face from his army days. I was fascinated by a stamp collection which he brought out at weekends; and his album of photographs of foreign lands and unknown comrades in the war. Father's presence was imposing and experienced with fascination. But in the face of his masculine intrusion, mother was the reference point. How she spoke of father, how she represented him, was crucial.

In the lower middle-class family, a mother has a particularly significant relationship to her son. She stands between him and his father, and colours his vision of the masculine world. The importance of her position is confirmed by a middle-class 'family culture', of which she is the principal representative (typically, her life derives its meaning from the domestic world); and through which she projects an image of paternal masculinity (partly presenting an ideal for her son to follow, partly defining him as he feels himself to be). The boy's gender-identification is immediately caught up in a structure of family relationships – a 'family tree' – with its own history and cultural continuities. With its stress on collusive solidarity – 'pulling together' through adversity – the family sustains a whole mythology, with which mother, especially, identifies.

In my own family, the ideal representation of masculinity is contained in my mother's account of her grandfather. This is repeated as a source of moral authority, by which to judge a changing world. Here are some extracts from an article about him which appeared in 1937, in the local newspaper, and which remains a family text:

'Most people who knew him were amazed when we stated last week that Mr. Arthur Gaunt had celebrated his 80th birthday. Most people would have said he was at least 10 years younger. Mr. Gaunt is a life-long teetotaller and non-smoker – and temperate in all things – and he believes that this, coupled with the fact that all his life he has been a good walker and done plenty of it, has contributed largely to his longevity ...

'As a boy he walked to and from his work at Armley, and

later he worked for a year at Bradford, and again he had to make the journey on foot. Apart from that, for nearly 50 years he has walked daily from Messrs. Salter and Salter's works on Lane End to the shop at Chapeltown where he was a manager.

'Mr. Gaunt started working half time in the boot trade when 9 years old ... making boots for Elijah Gledhill's at Armley. When 11 years old he went to Gledhill's at Armley for 2s 6d a week, and later started with Messrs. Scales and Salter, Pudsey, as a boot finisher. Subsequently he became a clicker and then a rivetter. The firm were then at Lidget Hill, and employed over 300 hands. Boot making was a flourishing industry in Pudsey in those days. Now there is not a single boot manufacturing firm in the town, the last being Messrs. Ogden's at Grove works.[5]

(*The Pudsey News*, 1937)

The article has two more paragraphs about Mr Gaunt being a long-serving committee member of the Mechanics Institute and one of the pillars of the local Methodist Church: '30 years as treasurer of the trustees, Sunday School secretary, trustees secretary, and Sunday School teacher ever since he was 20 years old. For many years he walked from Chapeltown to Lowtown and back 3 times every Sunday.'

Into today's world Arthur Gaunt brings three traditional patriarchal values, shared by his generation, but to be contested by his sons. First, he speaks about work, a life-time of hard work, the cornerstone of a man's moral dignity, and his major effort in life. Second, he speaks about promotion, about rising in the world. It is decisive for the history of my family that Arthur Gaunt rose, by his own diligence and effort, from being a skilled artisan to being a shop-manager, and thus a member of the lower middle class. His daughters became teachers, his son (my grandfather) an office clerk – children who nevertheless remained close enough to the working class to value their distance from it. Third, the old man speaks of 'respectability', and especially of non-conformist morality. His work and his promotion are justified by his temperance, and his belief in a higher duty. His dignity is founded on the assumption that in this

27

provincial Yorkshire town, everyone else shares his view of the world.

In some respects, of course, this definition of masculinity – worker, teetotaller, pillar of the church – was nostalgic even at the time it was written. The interest in dying trades, the very 'newsworthiness' of the man himself, testify to this. But the memory of Arthur Gaunt has been kept alive through the language of family reminiscence, in the supposed inheritance by children of their forefathers' characteristics, and in stories of the gatherings of long ago. These accounts comprise the family culture that has predetermined my own experience, and, in particular my response towards my father. The values represented by this successful manager are still, instinctively, part of my masculinity.

In this way, historical images of masculinity cut across a boy's gender identity. In the world of the family this identity is filled out, and begins to assume definite boundaries. The particular complexity of the masculine identity stems from the fact that an initially ambivalent response to the father is itself over-determined by a family culture, mediated by the mother. A boy is thus caught in a confusion of illusion and reality. Straddling a gulf between masculine and feminine interpretations, he is forced to contemplate idealized visions of his future: 'What would you like to be when you grow up?' The boy's world is full of promise, hope, anticipation; but it is a fantasy-world, which exploits his masculinity. Perhaps this is why so many men learn to exaggerate their own success: heroes in the end die hard.

There are, of course, different kinds of family culture, and variations of masculinity between different social classes. The lower middle-class image of patriarchal authority – based on moral dignity and 'respectability' – remains socially influential; but within the working-class family it constitutes a distant reference, an imposition, rather than a coherent family mythology. Working-class families maintain collective memories of poverty, and physical insecurity, rather than a nostalgia for Victorian provincial life. And working-class masculinity is characterized more by an immediate, aggressive style of behaviour, than a vision of personal achievement.

Here, for example, is how one man described to me his childhood in an old working-class district of Birmingham:

'All I can always remember is the beer, the parties, the fun, the rows, the arguments. 'Cause they was always there you know, night after night, week after week. There was always summat going on you know, nearly always fighting, and arguing about it. There's nothing that really sticks out. It was just the normal family life you know. There was five lads, three girls and Mum and Dad. It was hectic. Well four of us were sleeping in the same bed, the four lads you know. We never really got away until we all got married. Up till then it was always full, packed out.'

The claustrophobic atmosphere of the working-class home is reflected in the solidarity of its family relationships. Until their own marriages, individuals are bound within the ritual drama of family life. One feature of this drama, in traditional working-class neighbourhoods, is the close interpenetration of family affairs and the life of the street; and at the centre of this negotiation between public and private worlds stands the authoritative figure of the father. It is his paternal presence, in domestic arguments and neighbourhood violence, that primarily shapes the consciousness of the growing boy:

'It was a very friendly atmosphere and quarter, but as I say from what I can remember, what with the fighting and that that used to go on, my parents never used to bother. We never had people come. We lived in an entry which had ten houses and at some time or other Dad had belted every one of the husbands up and down the entry. There was no hopes of being friendly with them ... But I never got that involved 'cause I was too little; I mean I got shouted at and told to go to bed, and was up all hours of the night listening to the arguments, and lay crying in bed 'cause Mum and Dad were having a row, you know, and things like that. But I never raised my fist in the house.'

As this account makes plain, the intensity of working-class relationships is frequently disturbing – a far remove from the harmonious picture of 'working-class community' so often portrayed by sociologists. And part of the currency, the language, of these relationships is a particular 'masculine style'. As provider and protector, the father strives to defend his personal dignity at work and to maintain his authority at home. His presence is emphatically physical, in the 'straight-talking', 'rough and ready' way he behaves. There is a fine line, relating this 'normal' masculinity with the threatening 'front', the drunken violence, that is a man's last line of defence:

> 'Dad had been a PT instructor in the army, and, but then he'd got to have a drop of beer, he used to put us through PT of a night, perhaps till two, three, or four o'clock in the morning. And we used to be over chairs, over the table and under it, wrapping ourselves round the chair without touching the floor, picking 'em up on one leg, all things like that. And we used to play darts and dominoes. I always used to sing to him 'cause I used to have a nice voice in them days you know. I used to sing to him especially on a Sunday, being at home. As I say we had some good times, but it was hardly ever if he had the beer.
>
> 'When he was sober he was a perfect gentleman, but when he was drunk he was a bastard. I mean, you know, people think the world of him sober, till he's had a drop of beer. Then he's a different man altogether. You know he's a fighter ... He's rough and ready, he's straightforward, he'll tell you what he thinks, and that's it.'

In the working-class family the boy's ambivalent feelings towards his father are more or less directly experienced. Father is both 'a perfect gentleman' and 'a fighter' – the two faces of his 'straightforward' masculinity. Again, this ambivalence is structured by the masculine experience of work; the perception, within the family, of the father as worker. The frustration of his working life leads the father to insist on 'compensations' from his family: shows of support and deference, certain symbolic attentions (the old 'pipe and slippers' routine). But this formal insistence on masculine status is always contradicted by the indignity of wage-labour. At bottom (and this is understood by his family) the worker is individually powerless, a mere calculation of the capitalist economy. This remains the unspoken truth of his masculine identity. At home the working-class father is under continuous pressure to appear competent, to 'be a good father'. But his aggression, his bitterness, and often his violence, point to the impossibility of his situation.

Together, familiar perceptions and experiences make up a particular working-class emphasis, in the way 'masculine presence' is defined. The working-class boy is directed, not so much towards visions of inheritance as towards a daily routine of hard work. He learns, not a coherent family mythology, but a defensive language of 'compensation'. These are class differences in masculine identification which cannot be minimized, for they constitute one basis for the variation in masculine styles. They contribute to the underlying distinction between class cultures in capitalist societies.

Still, however, behind class differences in masculine behaviour, there persists an essential continuity. What working- and middle-class boys have in common is the masculine emotional structure – the basis of all subsequent personality development. Whether it is in terms of self-motivated ambition, or aggressive authoritarianism, the masculine personality is commonly built upon an ambivalent relationship with one's father; and I have tried to show how this 'ambivalence' follows from the identification with work – with father as worker – and the specific ways in which work is socially organized. For both classes of men, far from providing a challenge to the organization of work, their masculinity actually supports it, and helps it to continue. Masculinity involves making personal compromises with social problems – defending male prerogatives in the family, keeping up a 'front' against confrontations. Such personal 'solutions' are socially functional, because covering up for weaknesses, 'making the best of a bad job', is always to accept the status quo.

I shall return to this argument in later chapters; for it is the essence of the masculine problem. Here, however, it is important to recognize that men first learn their conservatism, as sons confronted with fathers, in the cultural world of the family. In all social classes becoming a man involves striving to go beyond, and yet intuitively accepting the imagined world of one's father.

It is in this sense that however much he strives, a boy must remain for ever fixed upon, subservient to, the sense of inevitability his father's authority represents:

'... the political and economic position of the father is reflected in his patriarchal relationship to the remainder of the family. In the figure of the father the authoritarian state has its representative in every family, so that the family becomes its most important instrument of power.

'The authoritarian position of the father reflects his political role and discloses the relation of the family to the authoritarian state. Within the family the father holds the same position that his boss holds towards him in the production process. And he reproduces his subservient attitude towards authority in his children, particularly in his sons.'

(Wilhelm Reich, 1972:53)

At play, and among his peers, a boy's emerging masculine identity is gradually institutionalized. The ambivalence of childhood crystallizes into a pattern of masculine experience, which both reinforces the underlying emotional structure and provides a direction for the future. Masculinity becomes conscious – an explicit system of taboos and recognitions of status. In groups boys devote themselves to the testing of masculine prowess – in fights, arguments, explorations of the local neighbourhood – and there is a complex boyhood culture of mutual challenge. Boys also learn a masculine language, which prescribes certain topics (sports, machines, competitions) and certain ways of speaking (jokes, banter, and bravado). This informal culture of the peer-group interacts with, and sometimes explicitly counteracts, the formal culture of the school. In its encouragement of competition (success and failure) and hierarchy (duty and reward), the state education system itself cultivates aspects of boyhood masculinity.

To some extent, this 'socialization' is a universal process of learning and adaptation. In all societies children inherit the world of their parents and are obliged to assume its beliefs and institutions. Part of a child's necessary education is some interpretation of biological reproduction, sexual difference, the functions of the body. In all human cultures the body is an important focus of play and a source of symbolic meaning. But societies differ in the amount of flexibility they allow to gender-identification and the particular ways they institutionalize sexual difference.

Feminist writers, like Ann Oakley and Lee Comer, have argued that in our culture, and especially for girls, the process of gender-identification is particularly stereotyped. Sexual difference is socialized into 'gender-roles' – which envelop individual lives. These roles are played within social groups, to which are attached 'scripts', or ways of speaking. The whole world of childhood, both inside and outside the family, is oriented towards the confirmation of gender identity, and children are forced to learn appropriate forms of behaviour – reinforced by toys and games, children's stories, parental attitudes, teachers, peers, and the mass media. A specific part of this socialization is the affirmation of masculine prestige. But this, even whilst it supports a boy's self-confidence, prohibits his exploration of alternatives:

'A girl may refuse the constraints of femininity during the period of childhood which the psychoanalysts have called "latency" – that is, between the ages of about seven and eleven. She may climb trees, play football, get into scrapes and generally emulate acceptable masculine behaviour, but only *on condition that she grows out of it*. No such tolerance is extended to the boy. He can never, even temporarily, abdicate from his role ... it is always the boy who represents the exciting and the desirable and to experience it, the girl has to identify with the male. The traffic is only one way, for while girls can cross the boundary to enter, for a short while, the company of boys, a boy may not join ranks with his inferiors.'

(Lee Comer, 1974:13)

By the time he enters adolescence, which will be my focus here, masculine stereotypes have become literally, a boy's 'second nature'. The appropriate model of gender-identification (footballer, fighter, man of action), now constitutes a basic image through which a boy expresses himself. Thus, the acute self-consciousness of adolescent sexuality is disguised by a

33

taken-for-granted masculine cameraderie. At school, or with his peers, the individual's insecurity is hidden by becoming 'one of the lads'. In the collective context a boy will reaffirm the chauvinist stereotypes. And against the inescapable reality of work, a conventional masculinity provides a kind of hollow reassurance.

School

Middle-class masculinity, throughout its development, remains oriented towards the culture of school. The ideals of achievement held out to the middle-class boy are usually defined in terms of academic success and the values of school are internalized by boys themselves. Masculine competence is expressed as achievement in sports or intellectual competitions. Male sexuality is discovered at school, with school-friends, and often through officially sanctioned activities : dances, societies, outings. Perhaps the cultural values of the middle-class family are crucial in supporting this orientation – books in the home, and parental help with homework provide a continuous emotional context for academic achievement. Certainly, in my own family, education was the first priority, and at the age of eleven I dutifully won a state scholarship to a local direct-grant boarding school, where I attended as a day-boy.

Though certainly not typical, my experience of school was socially indicative. For I belonged to that fraction of the lower middle class who, motivated by a surviving 'protestant ethic', made the most of the post-war expansion in education. The ideals of our parents were 'good qualifications', for 'respectable careers' – the guaranteed 'security' of a 'profession'. But the sons and daughters of northern provincial families were to find themselves moving away from their local areas, among cultural elites their parents had never met. As a 'scholarship boy', at a fee-paying boarding school, I was educated into an alien culture. Not only was I transported to a school across the valley, I also began to mingle with boys whose upper middle-class fathers owned the kind of small business in which my father worked.

The all-male boarding school was, of course, traditionally, an upper middle-class extreme. These schools transmitted, as a sanctioned part of their experience, a notion of 'manhood', which remained the ideological reference point for the training of 'gentlemen'. The desired qualities were personal endurance, an unquestioned devotion to 'duty', and an ability to administer justice (or punishment). Intellectual pursuits were held in contempt by boys with fanatically narrow horizons, chauvinistic loyalties, and conservative characters. Hints of non-conformity were suppressed by the boys themselves, and their informal culture was at every point bound up with, and supportive of, the ethic of the school. The following 'ten commandments' of the public schoolboy illustrate his approval of the institutional regime:

> 'There is only one God; and the Captain of School is His Prophet.
> My School is the best in the world.
> Without big muscles, strong will, and proper collars there is no salvation.
> I must wash much and in accordance with tradition.
> I must speak the truth even to a master, if he believes everything I tell him.
> I must play games with all my heart, with all my soul and with all my strength.
> To work outside class hours is indecent.
> Enthusiasm, except for games, is in bad taste.
> I must look up to the older fellows and pour contempt on newcomers.
> I must show no emotion and not kiss my mother in public.'
> (Alan Sandison, 1967 : 15)

At the centre of traditional middle-class education is an acceptance of hierarchy. At every level, the school institutionalizes a notion of 'privilege', tempered by 'duty' and 'service', supposedly inherent in the masculine character. A man is born to lead, but also, paradoxically, to serve those he leads. At the formal level this ideology is, I think, best summed up in the favourite maxim of my old headmaster: 'Privilege carries Responsibility'. The aim of the school is to develop an officer class (hence the prefectorial system, the house captains, the dormitory monitors, the boy scouts) but to moderate authority with a 'social conscience' (a charitable christian spirit). At the informal level, the ideology is lived out by the boys themselves, in an infinitely complex system of hierarchies which each boy must negotiate – before he, in his turn, attains the privilege of employing a first-form 'fag' to run to the tuck-shop. A boy learns which staircase is reserved for prefects, which outhouse for lower-fifth smokers. And above all, when caught, he learns to accept punishment without flinching.

A masculine emphasis to the principle of hierarchy is overtly encouraged. Masculinity enters into the process of 'character-building' – the notion that schools are not simply transmitters of knowledge: they carry 'traditions', demanding a personal sense of pride. Middle-class privilege is thus cultivated by a particular 'personality-type', typically presented in terms of an image of 'manhood' – vigorous, ambitious, quietly confident. To a large extent, 'manhood' in the public school meant an imperialist masculinity – the 'stiff-upper-lip' that built the Empire. No room here for sensitivity; the boy was brutally initiated into a sadistic culture of hearty back-slapping:

'In due course I was transferred to North. Then it was that I realized that the denizens of those frozen wastes were not, in fact, the coarse and brutal ruffians we of South had always considered them to be. True it was that we lived "on the top" three stories up, and slept with our windows open to the four winds of Heaven, so that the rain and snow used to blow in, and the temperature in Winter was often down to zero. True also, that we had no such decadent thing as a hot-water tap. We washed in cold water and revelled in it, and looked down on those lesser mortals, like those of South and East, who had hot taps. Then hadn't we our beam to jump? All newcomers had to stand on the casing over the staircase, and by a reasonably good leap catch hold of and swing from one of the beams which trussed the roof, falling ultimately on to a bed below, thereby proving their manhood, and fitness to dwell with the Gods of North.'

(*Woodhouse Grove School*, 1962:113)

This reminiscence of the school that I attended dates from the

1920s; and in a post-imperialist age there is perhaps less demand for such overt spartanism. The worst manifestations of brutality are certainly dying out, replaced by a modern sense of 'fairness' and 'responsibility'. But a middle-class education is still an education for leadership. There remain the prefectorial beatings, the system of 'fagging', and, naturally, endless rugby on winter afternoons. Even though, for most boys 'character' is now the exercise of 'initiative' in outward-bound courses, or the achievement of academic qualifications, there remains that certain confidence in oneself, that mastery of manners which 'maketh man', in the British ruling class.

In a single-sex boarding-school a boy's whole life is enveloped by institutional routine. His friendships are immediately part of the life of the school – the form, the 'dorm', a particular group of his peers; and they are regulated by the notion of 'manhood' which pervades there. The effect of this is to 'sublimate' a boy's emotional development; and the ultimate repression, in this context, is reserved for sexuality. There is, in the public school, an official notion of gentlemanly 'courtesy' and 'chivalry', practised in the formal mannerisms of the school dance or garden-party. The garden-party has the ritual grace of an Edwardian picnic – with over-dressed, poised young ladies, and worried, attentive young men. The girls are presented as adornments to the masculine scene: they bring colour and a joking embarrassment into the world of grey suits. In the midst of this performance an illicit sexuality persists – in images of romance and seduction. But in an exclusively masculine world, private fantasies can only surface as aggressive, tentatively homosexual, assaults in the showers, or in the lonely release of masturbation.

For all middle-class boys school provides a language through which they discover sexuality. Fathers do not (usually) talk to their sons about sex in the way that mothers (sometimes) talk to daughters. Boys find out about sex from their school-friends and friends provide an audience for accounts of sexual exploits. This means that sex is, from the first, part of the competitive boyhood culture, in which the insecure individual seeks confirmation in ritual jokes and cameraderie. Sexual experience becomes part of the hierarchy ('How far did you get?') in a series of gradations from 'just-good-friends', through the 'easy-lay', to ultimately 'going-steady'. Groups of boys develop conventions of sexual behaviour, partly dictated by teenage fashion (styles of clothes, dancing), but also expressive of masculinity (the 'pick-up', petting rituals, the bravado of possessing contraceptives). In all such activities, sexuality is part of a masculine advertisement – emphasizing self-possession and control as one manoeuvres to 'the point of no return'. The personal show of sexual competence is supported by an obsession with group norms – what everyone else is (supposedly) doing, 'am I doing it right?' And the group's communication is a self-sustaining network of boasting, half-truth, and fabrication, in which it is impossible to distinguish reality from fiction.

Whilst boasting of his sexual prowess, a boy still cherishes his personal fantasies of seduction. The ultimate step on the sexual hierarchy is a fusion of desire and wish-fulfilment in an aura of surrender:

> 'She is a mythical figure whom he has always been assembling part by part, quality by quality. Her softness – but not the extent of its area – is more familiar than he can remember ... The whiteness of her body is what has signalled nakedness to him whenever he has glimpsed a white segment through the chance disarray of petticoat or skirt ... This mythical figure embodies the desirable alternative to all that disgusts or revolts him. It is for her sake that he has ignored his own instinct for self-preservation ... She and he together are his own virtue rewarded ...
>
> 'He sees the eyes of an unknown woman looking up at him. She looks at him without her eyes fully focussing upon him as though, like nature, he were to be found everywhere.
>
> 'He hears the voice of an unknown woman speaking to him: "Sweet, sweet, sweetest. Let us go to that place." '
>
> (John Berger, 1972b : 108–9)

In the lives of adolescent boys, such fantasies provide a kind of 'magical resolution' to the daily drama of self-control. A stereotyped femininity is the idealized counterpart to rituals of chivalry and bravado. It is a fantasy of passivity: a woman's 'presence' is transcendental, beyond confrontation, and the stress of self-assertion.

What the dreaming attempts to conceal, but in its intensity also expresses, is a fundamental adolescent insecurity. This conclusion seems paradoxical – for boys are educated to be fearless, competent in a crisis, predisposed to adventure and exploration. But a masculine education drives a wedge between external behaviour and inner experience: the development of the former blocks the expression of the latter. There is, in the end, no recognized channel by which a boy can either communicate his feelings to others, or discover their possibilities within himself. In the masculine culture of the school, experience is 'policed' into a daily drill of 'character-building'; and feelings of tenderness, and especially sexuality, remain beyond recognition.

Because middle-class boys are brought up to accept them, the values of school exercise a powerful formative influence. As I have suggested, in his ambivalent attitude to his father, and in the complex emotional life of the family, a boy is predisposed to a life of competitive struggle. At school, through sports, exams, fights, and jokes, he learns to justify and to universalize this disposition – as a model for 'the way of the world'. The 'English Gentleman' remains, morally if not politically, at the summit of civilization. His manners, his sense of 'fairness', his devotion to 'duty' and 'service' together make up a socially legitimate character-type. Each aspect of this character supports the whole, in a 'balanced' network of 'qualities': 'judgement' is tempered by 'mercy', 'leadership' by 'responsibility', 'privilege' by a sense of 'honour' – and emotional restraint by fantasies of sexual reward. Institutional masculinity is like an internally-woven fabric; inside which a single-minded little man, restlessly struggling, spins his own cocoon.

And though it is in some respects anachronistic, a public-school education illustrates one significant, traditional form in which masculinity is institutionalized. Although the day of the classical public school is over, many elements of the model 'gentleman' survive. Competitiveness, personal ambition, social responsibility, and emotional restraint – these remain dominant masculine values in our society, which all boys are encouraged

39

to adopt. But it is necessary, also, to recognize an alternative to this tradition: the 'subordinate' masculine identity developed within the working class.

The peer-group

Not only in his perception of his father, but also throughout his boyhood and adolescence, the working-class boy internalizes a particular set of personal expectations. With the middle-class boy he shares the basic masculine character – a predisposition to assert himself, to compensate for an ambivalent identity. Like the middle-class boy he goes to school, participates in organized sports and competitive tests, accepts the institutional-ization of punishment and reward. But generally speaking, partly because of his involvement in the crowded worlds of family and street, and partly because he is usually defined as an academic failure, the values of school remain distant, alien, unreal. In his personal life the working-class boy turns towards the informal life of the neighbourhood – his masculinity is ex-pressed through the local alliances of peer-groups and street gangs. As he enters adolescence a boy knows the gangs, their leaders, the jargon, and ways of behaving, that guarantee his social acceptability. He expresses himself, not so much in an inner, compulsive struggle for achievement, as through a col-lective toughness, a masculine 'performance', recognized and ap-plauded by his 'mates'. The activities of his street gang range from 'just hanging around' to organizing petty crimes. The group oscillates between affirming itself, and extending its sphere of influence – through games of 'dares' and challenge. In retro-spect, these explorations of a collective identity, with their sense of adventure and high spirits, can be pictured as an heroic experience. One working-class man described to me the 'sheer devilment' of his youthful escapades:

'We used to go scrumping, pictures, plundering others when they had their bonfire night, and generally get into mischief, you know. They had me for breaking and entering when I was a lad: there used to be a nursery up by us on the Quinton Road, and when I was about, perhaps about ten, I broke into there one night and got caught. Broke into a factory, broke into a pawnshop – I got away with them, but I got copped at the nursery. I was taken to Ladywood police station for mischief and that. Then a bunch of us one day went down Gas Street to the canal, broke a barge from its moorings and towed that up to Selly Oak and they copped us trying to sink that, they had us in the police station again. Generally we were a load of mischief you know.

'Today? No. Scrumping today, to me, they don't know what it's about. Bonfire night we used to go plundering and rip old buildings apart, they don't today. They don't seem to have any spirit in them today. I mean all they're interested in today is fighting and cutting your bloody throat. We got into mischief and trouble, but certainly not gang fights and things like that ... It was devilment ... and at that age it wasn't malicious intent. It was just sheer devilment, you know what I mean?'

Boyhood is remembered as a golden age of freedom; when time was long, nights were warm, and the world, though infinitely detailed, was manageable. In the challenge to authority, the 'mischief' and the 'trouble', there was a harmony between personal identity and the collective 'spirit' of the group. But in this account there is also a sense that the atmosphere of the heroic world is gone. It has been shattered by social change it cannot comprehend.

Working-class gangs are based on mutual recognition. There are 'the lads', firmly located within a group's informal culture; and 'the ear-oles', oriented more towards 'respectability' at school and work. Within 'the lads', each individual has his place, which is ritually acknowledged. He may be introduced as a brother or friend, but he becomes a full member when he demonstrates a unique character, or special talents. He will then be recognized to be 'the brains', or 'leader' (initiator of activities), or a 'comedian', or simply the scapegoat, the comedian's victimized foil. Such recognitions of position are reaffirmed by periodic confrontations (fights mysteriously generated by the meaningful remark) and are continually supported by in-jokes, scuffles, and arguments. The existence of the gang itself is often the first focus of its activities, and its secrets are scarcely revealed to an outsider. From a few remarks made to me by a teenage member of a Black Country gang in a complex of council flats, I pieced together the following account:

'Me and my mates, we just hang about in the hallways, in the entrances, making a row, playing the Chinese man up. We're standing, just rowing, anything to start off. Victor would be getting punched and that. There are always fights with Victor. They don't like him 'cause he's big-headed. He broke his arm playing football – being big-headed he fell. We write all over the doors. Just put our names and "rule OK", "White-heath skins". And we take the doors down and play see-saws on 'em. We come here of a night to the disco, to the youth club. And we go to the Albion. We all stick together, don't matter which block we come from.'

By far the most important basis for recognition is territorial: someone who comes from 'round here'. Within the district as a whole, the gang's own particular locality is closely marked and guarded – often to apparent absurdity. In this account, the 'Harold Road mob' come from council houses on the same estate as the flats, and the shops ruled by 'the Oakham' are some fifty yards from the entrance to the flats themselves. For some reason however, they never transgress the local, territorial boundaries:

'Are you friendly with people in Harold Road?'

'I am now. Since they beat everybody up down on the estate. Now I'm friendly with 'em. You see they come down here and started our mate's motor scooter up, and they kicked our brother. They run us, that was it. They beat everybody up down the disco. One of their chaps started on this other chap, and the other chap ran on the stage, and they all went on the stage and kicked all the disco equipment up. They broke all the records and the record-player. It tends to be their disco. It's meant for everybody but it tends to be theirs.

'I mean, most of them come from round here. They just go in and look for trouble them do. They nick anything, cars and motorbikes and that. Break into houses, but not on Harold Road, 'cause they'd know who did it.

'Nowhere else to go. Nothing else to do I suppose. They're

older, about eighteen, but they just got the mentality of kids, they just do what we do down here ... Paul Bishop's their leader, 'cause he's the eldest. He's soft. He's been mothered a lot and he's really soft. But they all seem to take notice of what he says.

'The Oakham, they knife people. They don't come round here. They go round the shops.'

In this environment, masculine aggression is a fact of life. It is noticeable here that a boy speaks of becoming friends after a confrontation with his erstwhile enemies; that through 'messing around' he confirms his relationship to Victor, the gang's scape-goat; that he makes distinctions between 'trouble' involving doors and hallways in the flats, and 'trouble' at the disco, run by the church youth club. Aggression is the universal currency of working-class relationships, invested with a multitude of mean-ings. It is not, as some middle-class people think, anarchic, or meaningless. Aggression is the basis of 'style', of feeling physical, of showing feelings and protecting oneself.

The intense localism, and the aggressive style, shape the whole experience of working-class masculinity. For support and recognition, a sense of position and social status, the boy re-mains bound to the world of his neighbours and friends. In his emotional life, he is concerned with the physical presence he is able to maintain, as 'a force to be reckoned with'. He must learn to drink and smoke, and hint at sexual conquests. He does not actually need to 'prove himself', so long as he can return the banter, or hint at some skill or knowledgeability. For masculinity is more impressive played cool, in choice gestures and side-remarks, rather than in open boasting or violence.

In effect, working-class masculinity becomes a kind of 'per-formance'. As a boy grows up, tied to his particular audience, he develops a repertoire of stories, jokes, and routines. In his external personality, he learns to reproduce the expectations of his public – their inherited ways of speaking, their attitudes and values. Overwhelmingly, what characterizes his performance is a sense of 'fatalism' – of 'taking the world as you find it' – for inside the locally-constructed working-class world there is little room for individual deviation. Even in his personal experiences,

43

a boy is tied to the 'human nature' which binds his audience together.

In Jeremy Seabrook's *City Close-Up*, for example, two 'mates' discuss the pick-up scene in Blackburn:

'Ken: "(I was) about sixteen when I started getting interested in women seriously. But being with this lot here, well (*indicating Alan*) he was a bit of a rum'un before I met him. When you go around with him and his mates you can't help getting into it yourself. Even if you don't feel like it, you can't sit out on it quietly. You get a girl lined up, and you've got to go all the way or else you're ruined, you've had it, your reputation's gone ..."

'Alan: "... you work your way into it, you play around, and then you find your way into it. It's bloody normal. We're not sex maniacs ... You go out for a drink, and you expect to finish up with a tart, you know. Not just for sex, just to finish the night off. Make it a good night. It's only bloody normal." '

(Jeremy Seabrook, 1971 : 155, 157)

The performance of a successful 'pick-up' is the highlight of the masculine repertoire. It captures exactly the mixture of bravado, self-assertion, and collective recognition that characterizes a working-class adolescence. A boy needs to know the proper methods of approach, he needs the 'commonsense' that what he is doing is 'normal'. Against the possibility of a refusal, he requires the joking reassurance to be able to swear, to laugh away his failure. At the heart of a boy's experience there is an overwhelming pressure to conform: not only to the monotony of a working-class life but also, more significantly, to the routines of working-class culture. Of course, this culture has its strengths: in its localism and detail it provides a source of solidarity. But in its defensive conformity working-class masculinity is itself an imposition – inside the heroic world of boyhood there develops a fundamental compromise with the future.

The dramatic assertion of masculinity thus becomes an end in itself – always a suggestion, never a realization, of potential power. For a working-class boy, the paternal inheritance is blocked; it becomes a matter of frustrated compensation, rather than ambition or achievement. This masculinity becomes the 'front' by which a boy learns to mask his disappointments. Throughout his adolescence he comes to learn that heroic exploits are compromised: there is always an ultimate sense of futility. Perhaps this is why working-class masculine aggression often becomes a kind of 'cult', of 'machismo' or 'bovver' – the gratuitous violence which is so offensive to middle-class authorities. In essence, this violence expresses an inner desperation, a lack of self-confidence. The working-class boy is beginning to learn that he is part of a world which condemns him, inevitably, to fail.

In every society, the discovery of sexuality is part of a general process of social 'identification'. In Western, capitalist societies, with their extensive means of communication and with an advanced division of labour, 'identification' is a complex matter – involving the assimilation of many kinds of experience, ways of acting, and speaking. As I have tried to show, the formation of the masculine gender-identity takes place within three primary social contexts: family, school, and peer-group. As it develops, this identity is differentiated according to class cultures and different levels of social hierarchy. But the complexity and variation of this experience does not destroy the underlying continuity of gender. For boys masculinity provides a constant thread through a maze of childhood experience.

In our society, however, masculinity is 'institutionalized'. In part this simply means that gender, being socially defined, is learned through the institutions – family, school, peer-group – that organize everyday life. In this sense all social experience, in all societies, is institutionalized. But here, beyond the mere routine of everyday life, 'institutionalization' also implies a certain social *regulation*, even an *exploitation* of gender-identity. What is specific about our society is the way in which particular masculine ambivalences are systematically *reinforced*. In their explicit emphasis on 'masculine' qualities the major social institutions penetrate to the core of a man's personality. In so far as they highlight his frailties or insecurities they touch a powerful source of energy. By playing on personal weaknesses social institutions are able to enlist the emotional commitment of men themselves.

In the final analysis, 'masculinity' is a kind of cultural bribe. A boy's social commitment is won at the price of his independence – for which he is offered the empty promise of 'manhood'. The very notion of 'manhood' is internally paradoxical – offering a dream of fulfilment, on the condition that a boy submits to authority and convention. As I shall go on to describe, this paradox points the way to work, which then becomes a man's central experience. But in his education it means a constant show of competence, at the expense of sensitivity and feeling. The aggressive performance, and the avoidance of feeling (compounded by a constant need for social recognition), amount to a complex, self-sustaining syndrome. And boys continue to 'be boys' only because there is no escape from its hypnotic imposition.

3

The 'right' to work

'If you want to know a man, if you find him excellent, why you've got to have something to do together. You've got to work.'

(William Carlos Williams, *A Voyage to Pagany*)

For every man, the outcome of his socialization is his entry into work. His first day at work signifies his 'initiation' into the secretive, conspiratorial solidarity of working men. Through working, a boy, supposedly, 'becomes a man': he earns money, power, and personal independence from his family. The 'money-in-his-pocket' symbolizes a 'freedom' – to bargain and consume; and a 'right' to the respect apparently enjoyed by his father. More generally, through his work a man can feel himself 'extended' beyond his local horizons, becoming part of a vast economic organization. As a worker, the boy enters the market-place of negotiation and exchange. He is part of a collective masculine history, of confrontations and alliances, with its memories of war, depression, lock-outs, and strikes.

This masculine culture and history of work is supported by a personal commitment. There is a magnetism in the paternal birthright that transcends the daily monotony of wage-labour. As I have described, this commitment is developed within the family, in which the mother is at the centre. And in the domestic world father's economic power is enveloped by a mythology of work – notions of self-realization, and the 'dignity' of labour. Here, a boy learns a patriarchal language – a way of talking about work and the domestic economy – and this becomes his common-sense support for notions of masculine solidarity. A man will talk of the 'right' to work, implying that work itself is necessary for his psychological well-being.

The extent to which definitions of gender interpenetrate attitudes to 'work', is not often fully understood. For it is not simply that sexuality enters into the division of labour, differentiating 'men's' and 'women's' jobs. Nor is it a matter merely for legislation, to be reformed by 'equal pay' and 'opportunity'. For men, definitions of masculinity enter into the way work is personally experienced, as a life-long commitment and responsibility. In some respects work itself is made palatable only through the kinds of compensations masculinity can provide – the physical effort, the comradeship, the rewards of promotion. When work is unpalatable, it is often only his masculinity (his identification with the wage; 'providing for the wife and kids') that keeps a man at work day after day.

And though it becomes the basis for the whole of his adult life, a man's personal commitment to work, is by no means unproblematic. It is equally important to recognize that, because of the way it is socially organized, the experience of work poses a constant threat to masculinity. Here again we return to the central ambivalent structure of the masculine identity: though it is a man's destiny, work is simultaneously an overwhelming disappointment. In capitalist societies, with their highly developed divisions of labour, and the ever-widening split between 'work' and 'home', masculine expectations can only be maintained at the price of psychological unity. At work, a man's 'gender-identity' is no longer complete – it is slowly, inexorably, split apart.

On one level, the mere proliferation of specialized tasks begins to fragment the masculine experience. It determines, for example, the structure of state education: the division between 'arts' and 'science', the streaming, and the policy of failure. It is expressed in the way that work is physically organized – in the divisions between 'shop-floor' and 'office', or within the office, between 'management' and 'research'. His particular specialization means that a man can only have a superficial acquaintance with the working experience of his neighbour. Within his own world he is relatively isolated, condemned to a one-sided existence. This experience of isolation, of being trapped inside a particular skill or expertise, is especially acute for middle-class men – the 'experts', and so-called 'decision-makers'.

But a second, and more fundamental, threat to the masculine identity is posed by the very structure of 'work' in a capitalist society. There is a tragic irony in the fact that men themselves collude in supporting a capitalist culture of work which, as it expands, destroys its own human foundation. In essence, this is the observation pinpointed by the Marxist concept of 'alienation' – that the more men (or women) work for capitalist enterprises, the more the products of their labour (commodities) and the organization of the working environment (factories) take on an *alien* reality:

'... the worker is related to the *product of his labour* as to an *alien* object. On this premise it is clear that the more the worker spends himself, the more powerful becomes the alien world of objects which he creates over and against himself, the poorer he himself – his inner world – becomes, the less belongs to him as his own ... The *alienation* of the worker in his product means not only that his labour becomes an object, an *external* existence, but that it exists *outside* him, independently, as something alien to him, and that it becomes a power on its own confronting him.'

(Karl Marx, 1970 : 108)

As Marx himself explained, the experience of alienation is based on the hidden significance of the wage. By selling his labour-power for a fixed wage, to a capitalist concern, the worker allows his labouring capacity to be exploited beyond the wage's formal 'value' – a 'surplus value' is extracted by the concern. The products of his surplus labour appear to the

49

worker as something he has created which is then 'objectified' (as a piece of machinery) to be used against him (he is forced to work harder). In personal terms, the commitment of men to their self-realization is destroyed.

Of course, to some extent, the experience of work is an inevitable wrench away from childhood. 'Manhood' is achieved only at an emotional distance from the domestic world – as, physically, a man leaves home to 'go out to work'. But in capitalist societies a definitive series of cultural distinctions – between 'work' and 'home', 'work' and 'leisure', 'work' and 'life' – point to a major psychological splitting of the masculine identity. As Marx went on to express it:

> '... labour is *external* to the worker, i.e., it does not belong to his essential being; ... in his work, therefore, he does not affirm himself but denies himself, does not feel content but unhappy, does not freely develop his physical and mental energy but mortifies his body and ruins his mind. The worker therefore only feels himself outside his work, and in his work feels outside himself. He is at home when he is not working, and when he is working he is not at home.'
>
> (Karl Marx, 1970:110)

Once established, therefore, the masculine personality develops along an internal maze of splits and dead-ends. Men come to work with an ambivalent emotional structure, a subservience to authority, and a compulsive need for recognition. At work, they find their masculine expectations simultaneously confirmed (by a masculine culture of work, with patriarchal origins, and occupational roots), and denied (by increasing specialization and alienation). In addition to an institutionalized division of labour (with its fragmentation of processes and activities), the worker's own personal life is increasingly split (between 'work' and 'non-work' – or time spent away from the work-place). The initially ambivalent masculine identity is subjected to a daily routine of shifting experiences; but his submission involves a rejection of social alternatives. Fixed routines give rise to rigid, masculine stereotypes, defensively oriented against their own disintegration.

There are three phases to the argument of this chapter. In the first phase, and very briefly, I examine the historical inter-relation between cultures of work and masculinity – the patri-archal traditions of work and their transformation in capitalist societies. Second, I look in some detail at the two, principal, masculine character-types in our society: those of the working and middle classes respectively. The descriptions are 'docu-mentaries' of impressions and personal experiences, concluded by extracts from a longer interview with a man from each class. As these men talk about their lives, I hope that something of the inner structure, the texture, of the masculine experience may emerge. But as the final section emphasizes, this experience can never be finally formulated: masculinity has a historical development and is continually readapted to new social rela-tions. In post-war British society there has been a major shift in middle-class masculinity and an emergence of a 'progressive' middle class.

Patriarchy and capitalism

In several traditional occupations – such as farming, fishing, or mining – there have persisted forms of superstition supporting a masculine culture of work. This is an informal culture, often resistant to definitions of work imposed by the state, or by capitalist entrepreneurs. Its masculine prerogatives derive from a time when work was located within the family unit; when divisions of labour were organized as divisions of sex; when the 'husband' was not only the married man, but also the 'master' of the household. The mode of economic production (of agri-cultural produce and handicrafts) was sustained through familial social relations; the ownership of property was invested in the male inheritance. Strictly speaking, 'patriarchy' was the system of law and custom that maintained this inheritance; and it has been progressively undermined by capitalist property relations. But in spite of economic transformations and despite undoubted regional variations (in England with its highly centralized system of tenant farming, the patriarchal notion of the 'free-holder' was, for the majority of the peasantry, a distant ideal), certain elements of patriarchy have survived. Today their legacy persists in some 'residual institutions', and they are maintained as an ideology that continues to define men's personal aspirations.

In certain areas and occupations, patriarchal conditions of work have survived. In their study of peasant life in the 1930s in County Clare, Eire, anthropologists Arensberg and Kimball described how the activities of farming were supervised by the father/owner, on the basis of a sexual division of labour that assigned to men the heavy tasks and powerful economic transactions, and to women the upkeep of the household and the income from 'domestic' produce (such as butter and eggs). The father held his authority until he died, and he retained power to supervise the marriages of his children – involving the exchange of women, with their dowries, between the male inheritors of established properties. In such conditions, a son was directly dependent on his father. His education was directed towards his inheritance. The economic and legal ties which formed the filial bond were ritually maintained by a masculine community culture:

'The father does all the constant heavy work necessary to keep the land in so rainy and treeless a country. He makes drains, ditches, fences, walls, shelters and barns ... As the son grows older, he learns to help at these tasks, finally taking them over. The father prepares the garden, ploughs, plants and harrows, does all the spade work of cultivation and everything involving the use of horses and agricultural implements. The son soon learns that these are men's tasks, and he gradually assumes his share of them. The adult men of the neighbourhood rival one another at these tasks; they chaff and boast back and forth over their prowess. The son cannot fail to hear and value the techniques which he acquires.'

(Arensberg and Kimball, 1968:51)

But even where this 'ideal-type' patriarchal economy was supplanted, the masculine culture of work often remained. Within capitalist agricultural relations, where the worker was employed not by his father but by a tenant-farmer, and where, propertyless, he was 'free' to marry by choice, there co-existed customary sexual definitions of appropriate forms of work (with prejudicial repercussions in the definitions given to 'women's work'); and often, alongside the school, there remained an informal, traditional education into masculine skills and superstitions. In Ronald Blythe's study of 'Akenfield', a Suffolk village, a farm-worker and trade-unionist recalls his 'apprenticeship' in the 1930s:

'In those days, son followed father. That was the usual thing. So all of us boys followed father. Nearly all the village boys did this, we just had to watch and carry on. One or two broke away but it didn't seem a natural thing to do. People didn't ask a lad what he wanted to do when he grew up if they knew what his father did. You hear that farming was unpopular then but it wasn't deep down. We began watching at an early age; that was our training. I watched the shepherd and did what he did. He didn't have to speak very often, which was just as well as he was a man who liked to keep words to himself. They used to call him Old Silence.'

(Ronald Blythe, 1969:84)

Where remnants of patriarchal culture survived, the bond between son and father was reaffirmed by the work-group. The boy joined the world of men, and his membership was formally sealed through the 'initiation ceremony' – practical joking, 'debagging', and even forms of 'tarring and feathering'. Symbolically, the 'initiation' reaffirmed male solidarity in the face of a routinized world of drudgery and hard labour. Physical strength, the most basic of all masculine preoccupations, provided the central bond of recognition:

'It was often rough on the farm then. It was hell-fire and water for a young boy when he started work. The older men made it a point to be rough with the lads because that's how it was, that was the tradition ... The difference between a boy and a man at work is that although the boy is strong, he hasn't got the kind of strength to allow him to keep it up all day. It was this which the men used to mock when I was young.'

(Ronald Blythe, 1969:87–8)

Thus, particularly in rural occupations, rituals originating in ancient systems of production were only slowly accommodated to changing conditions of labour. They represented a sense of continuity, and had a vital emotional significance in the social confusion wrought by industrialization.

Over and above its survival in the masculine cultures of certain occupations, the patriarchal ideal has continued to define images of work, held by men themselves. At its most unconscious, a man's attitude to work reaches back to his identification with his father. As in my own family, the image of the father – and thus the notion of future inheritance – is crucially defined in terms of work. Mother is only being 'realistic' when she speaks to the child of father's status as the 'breadwinner'; for economic dependency on the wage-labourer is the material basis of the domestic relationship. Father's regular absence from the home, and his alien presence on return, are understood as somehow bound up with a mysterious power. As a child I remember visiting 'father's office' – a strange world of desks and papers, given, by his presence, a personal significance. And recollections of boyhood visits to father's workplace are a common feature of accounts of work experience – such as this reminiscence by the son of a miner. Thomas Jordan remembers visiting the pit with his father before the First World War:

'These excursions into the pit, along these grim galleries, awed me no end. The coal-seam was about five feet high. There were railroads leading into places where men hewed and filled the tubs coming along these rails ... My father had to go into each of these places to test for gas and for the safety of the roof. With only the two of us in the district, and nearly three miles from the shaft bottom, I did not feel very good ... The entire area was eerie but it did not ruffle the deep calm of my dad.

'When we got out of the pit-cage and directed our steps the short distance toward home, he always asked me how I liked the experience. Always I answered that I liked going into the mine which I did several times until I was fourteen years old. He was a fearless man and I did not wish to let him know that I was nervous or else he might have thought I was "queer".'

(John Burnett, 1974:102–3)

54

His perception of paternal competence – the authority of the strong, masculine exterior – shaped Jordan's sensibilities. As a miner's son with intellectual aspirations he was finally forced to break with the culture of the mining community: 'Among these lads I was light and frail, unfitted to compete with them in the field of heavy work ... Brute strength was needed and I had little of it. The goodness of my parents in bringing me up in the finer things was hardly the training needed for the rough and tumble of pit life' (Burnett, 1974 : 106).

A man's perception of his father stays with him all his life. In his own family he will reaffirm the patriarchal culture of his inheritance – his 'responsibility to the wife and kids', his ability to 'provide' and to 'be a good father'. So central are these notions that they seem to form a psychosomatic 'disposition' – not only influencing a man's social attitudes, but also shaping his nervous system and physical energies. Masculine models of behaviour – gestures, habits, tones of voice – become instinctive; and routines of work – schedules of activity and rest – make up the pattern of everyday experience. Even a man's sexuality is regulated by his basic commitment to work. And the complexity of that commitment is highlighted by the experience of unemployment, when a man's whole existence is thrown into crisis.

With the help of a working class informant, Dennis Marsden has observed that not just a man's 'self-image' but also his impulsive behaviour (the temptation of crime) and his sexual relationship with his wife, are affected by a prolonged period of worklessness :

' "I'm the type, if I've got nothing to do, I've got to have something to do. I've got to go out or somewhere. The last time I was out of work I got into trouble. You see, when you're out of work you start drifting, like. I pinched some cigarettes. You see, you can't afford anything, and I used to smoke about sixty a day when I was at work. Well it's to pass the time away, and for adventure as well. I've been tempted to do things like that, but you have to watch it. If you see things lying about, if there's anybody's door open and there's nobody in, like, I'm tempted to go in like." The marriage had run into difficulties, and the husband admitted privately that their sexual relationship had deteriorated during this first period of unemployment ... Later he made a point of telling us how his sexual relationship with his wife had improved since he had begun to go out and earn money again.'

(Dennis Marsden and Euan Duff, 1975 : 184–5)

From this account we can appreciate the profound inter-penetration of everyday routines ('getting out of the house'), personal habits (smoking and drinking), and intimate physical experiences (like sex) which comprise the 'deep-structure' of masculinity. 'Worklessness' involves a feeling of 'worthless-ness': a sense of failure, which cannot be rationalized away. Blaming oneself, it becomes impossible to look another man in the eye. The well-meaning question ('have you found a job?') sounds like an inquisition, and sympathy or reassurance carry undertones of insult. After a while a man begins to retreat from a continual confrontation with personal disappointment. The very foundations of masculinity – the identification with father, the patriarchal culture of work, the 'right' to work itself – are fundamentally undermined.

In contemporary societies, the experience of unemployment crystallizes the masculine predicament. For, in the context of its disintegration, it points to the ambiguous interdependence of patriarchy and capitalism. To some extent, because his identity remains the source of a man's motivation to sell his labour-power – capitalism reinforces patriarchal culture. Wage-labour offers to men a certain 'freedom' from the worst aspects of pre-capitalist economies (the personal obligation of the feudal serf to his Master; the life-time of unmechanized drudgery on the land). It appeals to a patriarchal self-image (the owner of private property is 'his own man') – an image which continues to find expression in a man's secretive attitude to his pay-packet. Peasants and agricultural labourers are still enticed from the land by the promise of material power which the wage symbolizes.

In *A Seventh Man*, his study of migrant labourers in Europe,

John Berger evokes the peasant's fascination with city life – so much of his attention is rivetted to images of consumer gratification:

> 'Those who have left and succeeded in the city and come back, are heroes. He has talked with them. They take him aside as though inviting him into their conspiracy. They hint that there are secrets which can only be divulged and discussed with those who have been there. One such secret concerns women. (They show him photographs in colour of naked women but they will not say who they are) ... What is not secret at all are the wages, the things to be bought, the amount that can be saved, the variety of cars, the hours worked, the arguments won, the cunning which is needed on all occasions. He recognizes they are boasting when they talk. But he accords them the right to boast, for they have returned with money and presents which are proof of their achievement. Some drove back in their own cars.
>
> 'Whilst listening, he visualizes himself entering their conspiracy. Then he will learn the secrets. And he will come back having achieved even more than they, for he is capable of working harder, of being shrewder, and of saving more quickly than any of them.'
>
> (John Berger and Jean Mohr, 1975:29)

The ambiguous nature of capitalist wage-labour is that while it reactivates aspects of patriarchal culture, it simultaneously seals their historical fate. Capitalism has its own laws of development, which run against the self-images of workers. In the first place, the mechanization of labour in extensive systems of production deprives the worker of his involvement with the materials of work. With automation, or semi-automated production, the finished product can no longer be surveyed as a monument to the human labour involved. Advances in technology also require a formal education, which tends to destroy the verbal customs handed down from father to son. The division of labour between factory and home threatens the authority of the father – his position at work is invisible, his 'protection' no longer direct. As capitalist organization undermines the traditional economy, the worker himself becomes

57

aware of a contradiction: that his wage, in effect, makes him powerless. In the eyes of his employer a man is not seen as a human being – with responses, aptitudes, talents, etc. – but as a unit in the cost of production; regulated to maintain profit margins. The bribe of 'freedom' begins to destroy a worker's self-respect – in the midst of a confusing world of half-truths in which he can only recognize fragments of himself:

> 'He begins to watch his arm, as if it were being moved by what it is holding instead of by his shoulder. He thinks of water pumping his arm. The moving pieces shift his eyes, the air breathes his lungs. In places liquids ooze out of the machine like the liquid that gathers round a fish's mouth when it has been taken out of the water and has stopped thrashing. He knows that what he is doing is separate from any skill he has. He can stuff a saddle with straw. He has been told that the factory makes washing machines.'
>
> (Berger and Mohr, 1975:99)

The experience of masculinity can only be understood in this contradictory context. It is this crisis of reversed expectations, and personal humiliation, which gives meaning to 'alienation'. Because he works for capital, the worker is alienated from himself. He consumes the rewards of his labour simply in order to go back to work next day. He is faced with an expanding system of production which undermines all he has learned from his childhood; and the more he exercises his 'right' to work, the more his product is used against him. It becomes more and more impossible for the worker to identify with his work. He is reduced, finally, to living for 'pay-day'; for the end of the week – the moment when, with the money in his pocket, he can drink to forget the monotony, collapse before the TV, or reassert, in a few hours of 'leisure' his dreams of 'independence'.

Working-class masculinity

The paradox of masculinity at work is most apparent within the experience of manual labour. For the manual worker there is an immediate alienation (his product is 'objectified' against him) and a direct, personal humiliation (constant confrontation with authority). But it is also primarily within the local traditions attached to forms of manual labour that elements of patriarchal culture have survived. Because of the often brutal and unpredictable nature of the work, the worker is directly dependent on 'masculine' compensations, and in some situations, patriarchal aspects of working-class culture may even be potentially subversive. A male chauvinism of the shop-floor is a way of asserting collective control, and, sometimes, sabotaging the production process itself.

Manual labour is collective labour: it is necessarily organized around the work-group. In part, this is simply because conditions of work are made more manageable by keeping a 'happy medium' with your mates. The individual contributes to a collective effort and the rhythms of working are reaffirmed by a collective culture – an 'occupational culture' (of jokes, gestures, the exchange of favours) on the job itself. To be 'one of the lads' is to be placed inside a group's informal boundary, to be a party to the symbolic play.

Thus, a man's personal experience of work is expressed through an endless drama of group interaction; and his social acceptability is defined in terms of his dramatic self-presentation. Formal definitions of status, and the type of interaction dictated by the technology of production, form the parameters of self-presentation. But these are filled out by a particular working-class sensibility; and it is his ability to share this sensibility that marks the 'insider' in an all-male work-group. To be accepted by his 'mates', a man must be able to recognize a network of group definitions: hierarchies of age (from apprentices to 'old hands'), of communities of origin (from immigrants to locals from various districts), and sometimes of 'gangs' or 'squads' – if men have some say in who they work with. In one Tyneside shipyard for example, these hierarchies form the basis for a whole 'style of conduct':

'What runs through all of these groups, and, from our observation manifests itself in most social contact at the yard, is a certain style of conduct. Certain topics of conversation constantly recur: current affairs, sport and sex. Persistent awkwardness or ignorance incurs a social penalty. The possession of a wide range of knowledge and the ability to handle well the style of conversation with its emphasis on quick wit, quick verbal reactions and rapid changes of tack, carry a social reward. To be regarded as a "character" or a "patter merchant" with a witty, caustic and self-mocking style and a wide variety of interests and stories is to have a welcome and an acknowledgement, in all parts of the yard and often outside it as well. This style of conduct commonly involves an element of horseplay as well: mock fighting, mock kissing, mock embracing.'

(Richard Brown *et al.*, 1973 : 107)

Within this masculine 'style of conduct', sexuality is a powerful and dynamic force. Sexual behaviour provides an endless source of practical jokes, a basis for self-parody and 'horseplay', and an all-pervasive 'commonsense' denominator. In a Yorkshire woollen mill, Dennis Marsden has observed the significance of sexual language in the expression of working-class masculinity :

'Swearing and sexual conversation bound the men together. As a topic on which most men could support a conversation and as a source of jokes, sexual talk and gesture were inexhaustible. In the machine noise a gesture suggestive of masturbation, intercourse or homosexuality was enough to raise a conventional smile and re-establish a bond over distances too great for talking. It was questionable how far such comment sprang from the quality of a man's life and feelings. It would be impertinent, on the strength of only an hour or two's conversation with a man to say anything on this point. But as with joking, so with "sex"; the conditions of life in the mill were such that some men's need for a quick joke or sexual remark became almost compulsive.'

(Dennis Marsden, 1968 : 75)

Marsden rightly comments on the circumscribed nature of sexuality at work. It is a formal, highly stylized, symbolic exchange. But beneath its conventional surface there is a deeper, psychological dimension. The manual worker needs the support of his work-mates against the feeling of being 'taken-for-granted' which the factory symbolizes. Without this defensive, cultural shield, a man would be too directly exposed to the humiliation of his position. The significance, in this context, of sexual symbolism, is its ability to unite the collective and the personal – to provide both a continuous diversion, and a psychological defence. In its repetition it points to an underlying insecurity; the seemingly innocent jokes have a force they cannot control. It is as if the worker despises his own sexuality – in the same moment as he reaffirms his commitment to work.

In the following account from a skilled tradesman (a Birmingham butcher) a certain masculine pride in his job exists alongside a brutalized sense of humour:

'All butchers are the same. You get them in the same crowd, the usual subjects – sex, women, you know. We talk in backslang all day long. I mean to say I could talk to you in backslang and you wouldn't be able to understand a word I'm saying ...

'A girl might possibly walk past, around twenty-two, twenty-three. She's wearing a big pair of breasts on her. Well what we say is (in back-slang) "look at the girl with the big breasts" ... I mean to say if I get an awkward customer, and you'll be serving her, she starts mucking about with you – this doesn't satisfy her, that doesn't satisfy her. You turn round to your mate and say, "She's a right old deelowoc that one." Well, "deelowoc" is an old cow. DLO=OLD; WOC= COW. You can rattle away all day and call 'em what the hell you like. A lot of green-grocers can speak back-slang, like they do at the market. They've got their own language down there ...

'Sometimes the carters will come round the shop like with the meat, and they'll come up with a real filthy book. And I'll read one of them – but if you've read one of them you've read the lot like, they're all the same damn story in any case. Some of the bloody things they bring, they're terrible they are ... They'll bring them and say, "Right, I'll see you in a couple of day's time when I bring the next load, and let's have them back." We look at them in the shop you know; really filthy bloody photographs.'

' "You don't bring those home with you do you?"
'Good God, not bloody likely! No I just look at them in
the shop for a laugh, and stick them in the mess-room.
'These are the sort of things that go with the butchering. I
mean to say if you haven't worked in a butcher's shop you
don't know what it is. As I say, half the time we spend looking at the women walking past, and talking about them. The
other half we're serving the rest of the customers like, you
know. Sex comes into it all day long. It's just one of those
things butchers are well known for. I don't know why.
Whether it's the smell of meat, or handling the meat or not,
I couldn't tell you. But they're well known for chatting the
birds up and one thing or another.'

Such accounts raise ideological and political questions which
are far from easy to answer. At some point the good humour, becoming an end-in-itself, obscures awareness of the conditions
it is intended to mediate. Against his conscience, the worker is
exploited by pornography ('really filthy bloody photographs');
and his everyday chauvinism reinforces sexual prejudice. The
butcher belongs to a trade with patriarchal traditions – a close
connection with farming and the countryside – and he can only
lament the passing of the old stock-markets, and the petit-
bourgeois shopkeepers. His lamentation turns to a reactionary
fondness for the 'natural' order of things – the small community,
the traditional family, the butcher, and the housewife.

However, in contrast to the isolated tradesman, Huw Beynon
has described the development of shop-floor action at Ford's,
Halewood. The power of shop-stewards to extend the scope of
resistance to management was rooted in the support of 'the
lads' of the work-group, and the union was ultimately dependent on rank-and-file support. To maintain their power the
stewards had to show a commitment to the lads, to their language and informal political style. Out of this situation evolved
a working-class politics not of rhetoric, or formal debate, but
of the mass meeting – with dramatic gestures such as the mass
walk-out, the march to the foreman's office, parodying formal
procedure. The negotiating style was based on bluff, spiced with
traditional 'scouse wit'. In the final analysis the lads themselves

possessed the power of sabotage, based on their own intimate acquaintance with the workings of the line:

' "In 1967 Bert Owen was the steward for the Wet Deck. The lads on the Deck played in a football team, went away on coach trips, drank together in the pub. They had their own nicknames for each other. A lad called John Dillon worked there. So they all took Magic Roundabout names. Dougal, Florence, Zebedee – 'Did you see it yesterday?' 'It's clever mind – how they do it.' There was also Mumbles, Big Ears and Uncle Fester. And Bert. They sang songs. Played about.

' "If there was a problem on the Wet Deck, a manning problem, speed-up, if the foreman had stepped out of line, they always had a comeback. They could sand the paint off the style lines – the fine edges of the body that give its distinctive shape. And nobody could know. The water streaming down, the whirlies flying about, the lads on either side of the car, some of them moving off to change their soaking clothes. The foreman could stand over them and he couldn't spot it happening. Three hours later the finished body shell would emerge with bare metal along the style lines." '

(Huw Beynon, 1973 : 140–41)

In this situation, a seemingly anachronistic working-class masculinity continues to have a vital political role. Because it provides a basis for collective solidarity, the culture of the work-group acts as an important form of resistance. The shop-floor is concerned to attack relations of authority, and point to the fact that a formal negotiating power presents only a limited challenge to the discipline of automated production. As car-workers especially have discovered, the jokes, games, and rituals of the work-group help to constitute an effectively localized power.

The dramatic expression of masculinity at work is thus part of a complex and contradictory situation. It is one feature of the familiar social world, and so constitutes a source of acceptance and recognition. Here, a working-class male chauvinism testifies to the personal experience of 'alienation'. However, underlying the particular work experience, the language of masculinity contributes to a supportive, working-class culture, capable of local resistances, and even of subversion. The richness of this culture – its flexibility and spontaneity – has only recently become apparent to middle-class eyes. In this context working-class male chauvinism is part of an elaborate symbolic world; and, in an age of mass-production, is a vital cultural defence.

But in making any *political* assessment of working-class masculinity, it is necessary to take a broader social perspective. Because of the centrality, in the lives of working men, of the shop-floor 'struggle for control', and because of the power of men in the family and community, the masculine rhetoric of the work-place comes to dominate every aspect of working-class politics. It is enshrined with the Labour Party and the Trade Union Movement – a language of 'brotherhood', a preoccupation with the 'right to work' and an emphasis on wage-struggles ('a fair day's work for a fair day's pay'). The resistance to managerial proposals for 'rationalization'; the concern to 'maintain wage differentials' for skilled workers; the insistence on lines of demarcation between connected processes – all reflect, in the first instance, *masculine* sectional-identities. The focus of such working-class politics is a defensive struggle for survival by the exploited working *man*.

Not only the official rhetoric of working-class institutions, but even the political ideals of men themselves are shot-through with this masculine emphasis. It is not simply that his 'family background' and education will influence the way a man votes – it is that his political vision, his conception of what is socially possible, is constructed out of his patriarchal inheritance. Huw Beynon's account of political struggles in the Ford Motor Company contains a significant observation. In the Halewood plant, trade-unionism, class-consciousness, and patriarchy went hand in hand:

'All the stewards were the sons of manual workers, and well over half of them (twenty-one) thought their fathers to be "strong supporters of trade unionism". The heritage is handed down from father to son, to be remembered and fought for again ... The process is complex and troublesome. Sons rebel against their dads and what their dads stand for. But what is guaranteed in this process, is that the sons are aware of ideas which explain society in terms of opposed classes and these ideas can be turned to and called upon to interpret future situations.'

(Huw Beynon, 1973 : 190)

It is important to recognize the significance of working-class politics in demanding 'capitalism with a human face'. But where definitions of class struggle – the future of the class as a whole – can only be conceived in masculine terms, resistance is inevitably partial. There have been two main political consequences of the working-class masculine tradition. First, it has systematically discriminated against women and children – both in its lack of attention to problems of the family; and in its prejudice towards working women. The 'class struggle' has supposedly been fought 'on women's behalf' by men, and class 'solidarity' restricted to a politically-conscious 'vanguard' of male workers. Second, in its own terms, 'masculinity' has inevitably involved political compromise. For the traditional masculine attitude to the family has demanded a certain social stability, a fatalistic adjustment to a commonsense 'reality'. With 'a wife and kids to support' the boat cannot be rocked too drastically.

It is this second point that I want to emphasize here. For I am arguing that over and above their sexual exclusiveness, masculine politics are ultimately prejudicial to working-class men themselves. Because they carry over, into the family, a male-chauvinist working identity, working-class men make particular demands of their 'non-work' experience. They are supported at work by an idealized image of 'home-centred leisure'; a notion which provides wage-labour in the factory with its mirror-image. In part, the character of 'leisure' is materially determined by the wage form – a typical round of immediate satisfactions oriented towards 'pay-day'. But also, the institution of wage-labour ideologically requires the one-sided notion of 'independence' which, for a man, leisure in the home represents. As long as this definition holds, men within the work-group will tolerate alienation and exploitation. Wage-struggles and 'collective-bargaining' will be the extent of working-class politics.

65

In our society, the idea of 'leisure' has two main elements. First, and most obviously, leisure is 'free time' and so, within limits, in contrast to the discipline of work, it implies 'choice'. Here, his leisure represents to the wage-labourer a definitive expression of his 'independence'. Second, however, leisure is something to be 'earned'; work comes first, and leisure is the reward for effort. What a man does in his spare time, when he can 'be himself', is always to some extent 'achieved'. So leisure as a dual satisfaction – partly for its own sake, and partly for what it represents as a fulfilment.

But leisure-time also fulfils a basic economic function. It is a moment to relax, to unwind, making it possible for the worker to return to work next day. Home-centred leisure *is* 'freedom' and 'independence'; but it is also economically and socially *necessary*. Its ideological definition, as the ideal expression of the wage-labourer's reward, the antithesis to the alienation of work, rests uneasily beside this function in the *reproduction* of the labour force, where 'leisure' completes a social cycle which enables the capitalist economy to continue its relentless progress.

The idea of 'home-centred leisure' – bringing home the consumer goods, providing for the family – has become increasingly important in post-war British society. In certain highly automated, mass-producing industries (again the car industry is a prime example) there has been an 'industrial relations' exercise in the management of 'affluence' – the reward of high wages for soul-destroying work. It has even been suggested that the worker has a fundamentally 'instrumental' attitude to work – that is, that he works solely for money which he can spend outside the factory. If this were true, it would provide the perfect 'solution' to alienation at work. A man would simply turn off from the activity he performs for most of his life, and with the wage in his pocket, redirect his demands for emotional satisfaction to a 'privatized' social life at home.

Sociologists Goldthorpe and Lockwood, for example, have argued that:

'In consequence of the conjugal family assuming a more "companionate" or partnership-like form, relations both between husband and wife and between parents and children would seem more likely to become closer and more inherently rewarding; certainly more so than could have been the case under the economic and social conditions of the traditional working class community. If workers are better able to satisfy their expressive and affective needs through family relationships, it may be anticipated that (they) will less commonly regard their workplace as a *milieu* in which they are in search of satisfactions of this kind.'

(Goldthorpe, *et al.*, 1968 : 175–6)

But what this thesis of 'instrumental workers' – retreating from the 'community' to the 'home' – essentially takes for granted is an idealistic picture of the 'companionate' working-class family. It is generally imagined that in the widespread move from old slum areas to new council-housing estates working-class families have adopted 'expressive and affectionate' life-styles, able to balance neatly and 'compensate' the working man for his alienation at work. 'Whatever happened in the past,' claim Young and Willmott:

'... the younger husband of today does not consider that the children belong exclusively to his wife's world, or that he can abandon them to her (and her mother) while he takes comfort in the male atmosphere of the pub. He now shares responsibility for the number of children, as well as for their welfare after they are born.'

(Michael Young and Peter Willmott, 1962 : 21)

This pious, sociological portrait of the working-class 'conjugal family' has some surface credibility because of the undeniable post-war expansion of domestic consumption. Accompanying the move to new housing estates, a sparkling ideology of affluence has pinpointed the home as the symbol of economic status. By far the majority of consumer durables have been directed, as household gadgets, at 'the housewife'; but also consumerism has singled out the working-class man, and his interest in new forms of leisure. It has offered him the family car, the TV, and the do-it-yourself craze. Working-class men are increasingly placing 'home' – represented by soft light-

67

ing, fitted carpets, ever-present colour TVs – at the centre of their leisure interests. Away from the grind of production, there is more space, more money, more to do.

But it is debatable how far this management of domestic consumption represents a *new* departure for working-class family *relationships*. Indeed, the notion of a 'companionate' family life-style, in perfect balance to alienation from work, itself *reproduces* an entrenched, traditional masculine attitude to the family – that it be as far as possible 'trouble-free'. Typically, the working-class man views the world of the family in a different light to other social relationships. Whereas at work he is individually powerless, at home he has personal influence and recognition. He goes out to work for others (the 'wife and family') partly on the condition that they, in return, reaffirm his patriarchal status. Without the material benefits of food, sex, relaxation, and the psychological benefits of emotional support – there would be no point to his working at all. 'Status' at home means that a man is above the fights and traumas of family life. Despite the observations of Young and Willmott, the physical welfare of children is, in the final analysis, the responsibility of the wife.

In addition to the masculine status it provides, 'home' also represents privacy. Working-class people in cities, live in crowded conditions, and so it is very difficult to escape the public world of work-place and street. Despite a widespread nostalgia for the working-class 'community', therefore, there have always been invisible but significant boundaries between family and street. Neighbours are important, but not everyone is allowed across the threshold. Those who do, enter on the condition that they will recognize the prerogatives, in 'his own home', of the working man. Typically, neighbours do not call on Sunday, or at 'teatime', and they will recognize the importance of a man's right to his 'leisure'. 'Privacy' means that the world of work is forgotten; that the bond between a man and his wife is secretive; that there is a barrier put up by the 'respectable' family, between home and the outside world.

One working-class man who talked to me was quite explicit on many of these points. 'Work' and 'home' are, for him, firmly distinct. At home he values his marriage, and he paints – seascapes, rivers, and mountains – by himself, in his front room. He works as a van driver and delivery man; but without the family there would be little purpose to the daily routine:

'*What are the main responsibilities of being a family man?*'

'Providing, I suppose. Making sure you can provide as best you can. Never ever out of work, things like that you know. Go to work. Keep them in fact, as best you can. Try and tolerate as much as you can.'

'*Does your family occupy your mind very much?*'

'Most of it. They occupy it more than the work and more than the painting put together really. I mean, I think about painting more when I'm at work. I never think about work when I'm at home. I never think about work at all. When work's finished I've finished with it, you know.

'The family matters most. That's what it's all about. Nothing would be worth doing if it was not for the family. If I hadn't the family perhaps I wouldn't bother. I'd probably be on the dole – well, I wouldn't be on the dole, but I'd feel I might as well be. Because I wouldn't have to work, wouldn't have to do nothing really. Probably just bum around.

'So it's all for them. I can do anything when we're in harmony, but if we ever fall out over something I find I can't do things you know, or things don't go so well. It's got to be all right with the world sort of thing and you're OK. I don't like going to work after an argument. We don't argue that much you know. We don't fight at all. We have differences occasionally, that's about all. But I don't like going to work without seeing they're all right. There's nothing you can put before them really is there? Not really, no.'

For the working-class man, 'home' is thus a key emotional point of reference. Economic provision, relaxation from work, 'harmony' – these are the central values in a status-conferring world. But there are also half-admitted tensions, domestic problems, which a working-class man cannot bring himself to recognize. For the fragile masculine identity, the 'authority', and the ability to face work at all, would likely collapse: 'I'd probably be on the dole.' If there are arguments, a man cannot work. He has an emotional investment in the smooth running of the home. And as the resources of the family are stretched to the limit, there is a hint of defensiveness, of covering over the cracks: 'We don't fight at all; we have differences occasionally.'

Behind its 'harmonious' facade, the masculine attitude to 'leisure' creates problems for itself. 'Home' is seen by men as a *retreat* from the outside world; the needs brought home are bitter and insecure, overloaded with the desire for 'peace and quiet'. But the family, as an institution – crowded, emotionally charged, dominated by the needs of children – cannot easily cope with these demands. The limited resources of a marriage cannot simply 'compensate' for work, nor satisfy abstractly-defined 'expressive and affective needs'. More often, deeply troubled masculine feelings are swept away by feminine tension-management, and the cost of harmony in the home can be a masculine superficiality towards feelings in general, in relationships within the family, and in a man's relationship with himself.

For what is fundamentally at stake, in the working-class family, is a man's 'conjugal right' to reproduce the *authority* he faces at work. Because the insistence on domestic 'harmony' is, at root, a defence of male supremacy, the balance of a man's identity hangs upon the demarcation of domestic responsibilities. Any challenge to the status quo is taken personally, as a confrontation. And because, in its origins, the sexual division of labour is irrational, such a confrontation encounters deeply unconscious barriers of resistance. If a man cannot maintain the exclusive 'right to work', he faces the destruction of his position within the home. In moments of unemployment, or domestic crisis, when this 'right' is undermined, the balance of power in the home becomes a personal anxiety:

'Mr Vickers, looking back on his spell of unemployment after he had found work, admitted that he could never have allowed his wife to go out to work while he did the housework. "You see, I've never lost my, sort of, *manly status*, if you like. That's what he's done, isn't it, the bloke who sends his wife out to work. Fine, O.K., if it's the only way of providing a reasonable standard of living, and the option is for both of them to both sit at home on national assistance and both be even more miserable. But at the same time you would certainly feel – well, I would – I would certainly feel as though I'd lost a bit of my manly status." '

(Marsden and Duff, 1975 : 170)

Precisely because of the authority on which they insist, many working-class men remain, unconsciously, afraid. Obviously, to write about this is to move upon flimsy ground, for these feelings are not only unexpressed but also vehemently denied. But working-class men are, within their formal joviality and 'matiness', often alone. On a modern housing-estate there is no men's equivalent to the 'community of women', for the masculine culture of the work-place is kept as far away as possible. Domestic relations are supported by formalities and appeals to custom, for which the empty formulas of oral tradition all too readily suffice.

The working-class idea of 'being a man' thus demands a certain inarticulacy, or distance towards the complexity of personal experience. One man admitted his inarticulacy to me during a discussion of his parents :

'Although I don't see Mum and Dad you know, I do idolize them in me own way. But I can't really express the feelings. I can't really say how my feeling is, you know what I mean? Never been able to express feeling. People say, "bloody hard him, he's rough and ready", and all that. I don't think I am, but I've never been able to express feeling.'

Taken as a whole, then, the separate compartments of a man's life seem to confirm each other : 'leisure' is the counterpart to 'work'; the intimacy of the family balances the 'instrumental principle' at work. This apparent equilibrum is preserved, as I have argued, in masculine working-class politics – an emphasis on wage struggles to the exclusion of the domestic sphere. But beneath its formal structure, the 'masculine front' conceals the disillusionment of its emotional interior. In many working-class accounts of family life, there is a feeling of resignation which often seems to express mixed masculine attitudes of confidence and insecurity. In the barely-controlled aggression of the chauvinist style, there is an undercurrent of tension that must, it seems, explode.

Bill works as a lorry driver for British Leyland, and he is a shop steward. When I talked to him, in Spring 1975, the fate of the whole corporation was in the balance. Throughout the West Midlands men were faced with short-time and lay-offs, subjected to the dictatorship of a major capitalist recession. Proud of his working-class origins, Bill emphasized the centrality of work ('and when I say work, I mean work'), as a challenge and as a source of 'pride'. In a skilled job, the senses are tuned to a pitch of concentration; and the wage is a direct measure of achievement. But the impersonal context of factory production continually threatens a man's equilibrium: over his expectation hangs the threat of redundancy; beneath his political gesture lurks a sense of powerlessness.

As Bill himself indicates, the cornerstone of a man's working life is his family. As an educative force, and as the focus of his adult responsibilities, the family is a major source of personal ideals. It is notable that Bill introduces his experience of work by talking about his father: a difficult relationship is mediated by a common respect for 'hard work'. It is primarily through his early experience of his father's work-place that he gains the motivation to 'make something of himself' – to join the air force and become a skilled lorry-driver:

'I was brought up in a working-class family, with a working-class background, in Kings Heath, in Birmingham. Lived in a council estate. Very happy atmosphere, very great community spirit. Wonderful road to live in. It was one of those sort of old-time estates where everybody knew everybody else, and the front door was always open. You never used to lock doors, or anything like that – people used to come in and wander about. In fact, the best grounding any man could possibly ask for.

'Four sisters and myself, a very happy family. I was very close to my mother. Mother was a very gay, friendly, outgoing sort of person. The sort of person that the neighbours could always call on for favours. You know, Mother was always there. She didn't spare the rod, believe me she didn't spare the rod, but she was still a very warm and lovable person, you know what I mean? She'd do a thing and then feel sorry for it afterwards. She couldn't do enough for you, she was that sort of person. She was very proud of us all.

'My father was very strict. I must confess we didn't get on well together for a long time. I think he resented me going in the airforce after my mother died – didn't want me to go. But the one thing I will never take away from the man – he was a very hard working man. He worked long, unsociable hours. Never kept us short of anything, he was always very good to us in that respect. I suppose the main thing was a clash of personality. Perhaps it was my fault. He's a peace-at-any-price man.

'He was strict with me, and perhaps he favoured his daughters a little, perhaps I could say that. Perhaps I didn't come up to the expectations he wanted of me, perhaps that's what it was, I don't know.

'I went to George Dixon's grammar school. Now there's a shock for you – for a lorry driver. My mother died with cancer when I was fifteen; she'd been ill for several years previous to that. I don't use that as an excuse for my own behaviour – it may have been contributory to it – but I was a great one for playing "wag" – you know, truancy from school. I used to spend more time walking around town than I did going to school. I'm not proud of it, believe me I'm not proud of it. I'm just merely stating a fact.

'Now when my mother died I left George Dixon straight away, and went to work with my father in Kings Norton papermills. And when I say work, I mean work. This was a six-day-week, six in the morning till six at night, six days a week. So I mean, I started off knowing what work was about. In fact I went into the airforce to escape it. Not because I was idle or anything like that, but – OK it's a little bit of snobbishness if you like – I didn't want to be a factory hand all my life. I didn't want to just draw my wage packet, go out and get drunk, and come back next Monday and earn enough to get drunk the following Thursday. That's never represented enough to me. That's not life – that's existence.

'God knows, I have every sympathy for people who are forced into that. And people are obviously forced into that kind of environment, it's not their fault. But I was determined that I wasn't going to allow myself to be forced into that environment. I went into the airforce, and had an extremely enjoyable time in the airforce – I loved it. But of course, like most young men, towards the end of my service I used to see my friends spending wads and wads of money while I was only getting about £5 a week in the airforce. So I left the airforce and got a job as a bus driver. And that was really where the driving started.'

For Bill, driving is self-expression. In a certain sense, there is a continuity between the requirements of the job, and his own personality: the 'gypsy' in Bill's 'soul' prefers a life on the road. Here, he analyses aspects of this experience of work – feelings of 'independence' and 'pride'. As his own experience illustrates, work can be a total masculine commitment; making retirement an impossible readjustment of the 'pitch' of a working life:

'I suppose really I like the freedom of the job, in so far as once you're behind the wheel of a vehicle and you've been designated a destination, and a load for that destination, you are the master of your own destiny. You're not being harassed by foremen on the shop-floor, you're not having somebody standing on your shoulder. It gives you a feeling of, you know, independence to a degree.

'You've got to be ready for everything. Well, let's face it, there's no room for relaxation on a 32-ton vehicle. There's just no room to relax. I mean you're sitting there – OK sometimes you can afford to let your mind wander a little bit, you might be thinking about the egg and chips you're gonna have at the next stop – but all the time your mind is working. You have these big mirrors either side of you, and you have to use those mirrors. You've got to watch your speed because, let's face it, the police are very keen on heavy goods vehicles who keep going over the speed limit. You have a certain responsibility towards the motor itself as well, you're listening for any peculiar noises coming from the motor. You've got your brakes and everything. All the time you're working, you're never relaxed you know.

'You know it amazes me, the amount of drivers I've known who have retired from driving and died very quickly afterwards. Because I think, you know, that they have been keyed, or tuned rather, to a certain pitch. To a pitch where their bodies and minds were disciplined to total concentration. And then to suddenly have it all taken away. Nothing to concentrate on anyway, except pottering around in the garden, or letting the pigeons out, or something like that. I can give you cases at "the Austin". I've known four or five drivers who I've known to be physically perfect. And they've retired, and six months later we've been having a branch representation at the funeral.

'There must obviously be, not just in transport, in every type of job, there must be a certain amount of pride. I mean, if there weren't any pride at all, the standard of that job would surely fall very quickly. And it is part of the pride that you maintain the standard of that job. You're proud to be a driver. Let's face it, it's nice to sit behind a big wheel and go bowling along the road. You know, you get the feeling, "Look, I'm somebody," you know, "I can handle this. I've got a heavy-goods licence, I can handle this vehicle." That'll be pride. You may not actually recognize it at the time, but if you really stop and think, and you're honest about it, you've got to admit it's there. Otherwise you wouldn't do the job properly would you? I mean you'd just bowl along and say, "Well, to hell with it, why should I worry? It's not my wagon, and it's not my car I'm going to hit, and I'm bigger than them anyway, I could roll over the top and not even get hurt." Can you imagine the sort of chaos that could evolve from a thought like that?

'I went into the Austin factory once. I'd been a coach driver. But of course the unsociable hours – when you're married you know and the first child's arrived. It was causing a little bit of friction obviously, family-wise, so I got out and I got this job in the factory, initially as a labourer. It was the only job that was available. I've always been able to say that any job is better than no job, you know what I mean? I would rather be in work as a labourer, than out of work as a Social Security number. And I worked in the factory. I would attribute most of what I know about the factory to when I worked inside the factory. But I couldn't get to grips with it, because I kept getting resurgences of what I was saying – this pride in being a driver. I used to watch people I'd worked with before bowling past "the Austin" while I was going to clock in and push my little truck about. Unfortunately it was a job that took place with a roof over my head. And having a little bit of gypsy in my soul I never came to terms with it. And that was it, I left, and went back on to driving – driving oil tankers, on contract to Shell at Blackheath.'

It is because of his involvement in his work that Bill resents the impersonal organization of capitalist production. As a shop steward, he is motivated by a commitment to 'humanity', against the anonymity of relations on the factory floor. He recognizes a generalized feeling of 'Them and Us': a gap, founded on 'ignorance', between the procedures of bureaucratic management and the 'voice of the shop-floor'. But at a certain point, although he is against redundancy in principle, Bill's social conscience comes up against the 'realities' of economic recession. Alongside a recognition of the falling rate of profit, his political faith is compromised by the masculine, commitment to working for a wage:

'British Leyland suffers from its size mainly. It's this corporate image you know – they've outgrown humanity. You know what I mean? There is no humanity left in the firm at all. The most common statement that you come across from the worker in British Leyland is that you're nothing but a clock number. Of course within the last few years we have established industrial relations departments, in an attempt to overcome this feeling of "Them and Us", which is the feeling of course at British Leyland: But I don't think they work because they are too management oriented. I don't believe that the unions, although they do try, I don't believe that they present their case as forcibly as the management do. I mean when the management want to produce a case, they use the national press to the fullest possible advantage.

'In the time that this "Them and Us" split has been allowed to develop the management have definitely encouraged this syndrome. Since when trouble arises on the shop-floor, the management then can divorce themselves from that problem and say, "Well, the problem is not ours; the problem is on the shop-floor." Well this of course is totally wrong because the problem is theirs. Anything that affects British Leyland is the problem of anybody who works there.

'My aim is maximum possible employment, and maintenance of a reasonable living standard. And believe it or believe it not, the continued affluence of British Leyland — because without that you can't have the other two, can you? You know, you read about militants. Well, I would be the last one to say there isn't militancy in British Leyland. Of course there's militancy. But militancy is bred through ignorance. A man who understands the true situation in British Leyland is not going to be militant to the point of bankrupting his own firm. You see, we have to accept that we have reached a situation where the world demand for cars has dropped off dramatically. And per capita, the profit on a car is virtually negligible now. Now we said that we would rather see short-time working than redundancy. Because it is obviously better, both for a man's dignity and a man's pocket, to be earning £40 a week instead of £60, than he be on the dole drawing £18 a week and being a drain on the country. This is what social conscience is all about, surely? At least, it is as far as I'm concerned.'

For the male wage-labourer, the threat of redundancy is a humiliation. As Bill puts it, unemployment strikes not only at the 'pocket', but also at a man's 'dignity' — the basis of his 'pride'. The emphasis here is important, for over and above its sheer economic necessity, the experience of working is at the centre of a man's social life. The wage, which redundancy removes, is much more than an economic 'wager' (the exchange of money for labour-power). Not only in its capacity to purchase, but also in what it *represents* (in the pub, or in the family) the wage symbolizes a man's 'social presence'. If his symbolic power is destroyed, a man's personality is undermined:

'If I agree to two thousand people being made redundant, that is throwing two thousand people on the dole. I would say that out of those two thousand people, probably fifty of them would think, "Oh yes, well this is a good thing on the dole, I'm not doing anything and getting paid for it." But I would venture to suggest that the other, vast majority, would feel a deep sense of injured pride. And let's face it, who's to say it's not a man's right to have a few luxuries if he can afford it? Well of course, he's brought down to dole money then. He's first of all to get rid of his car because he can't afford to run it; and I think you'll agree with me the loss of a status symbol can be a big blow to a man's pride straight away. And not having the facilities to provide for his family what he could provide before is the biggest drain on his pride. And this would be an argument I could use against redundancy. But you ask me if I think redundancy is inevitable at British Leyland and I say yes it is. I am caught between the two. I know that it is inevitable. I know that it is necessary. But I cannot in all conscience say that it is a good thing for the person concerned.

'I think the pride I'm talking about is the fact that while he may not do it consciously and openly, you know, flaunting his wealth or assumed wealth, the man who's well paid is proud because he's been able to provide his family with everything they want. His children go to school well dressed, well shod, they don't go short of holidays, they don't go short of the little things children love – like toys, bikes and such like. And to suddenly have these snatched away from him, and to have to turn round to that child and say, "Well, that bike has got to last you another two years because Daddy can't afford to buy you this"; or, "That pair of shoes has got to last you a bit longer" – it's got to have a terrifically negative effect on this man's pride.

'I mean it's such a sudden reversal as well. It's not a gradual thing. It's not a thing that a man can get used to. He's taken from one environment into another straight away. And I've seen men, believe me, who now come into a public house at twenty past two, knowing there's only ten minutes left, and they have a couple of swift halves, and they'll stand on their own. People who used to come and stand in a party say, and used to come in at one o'clock, on a lunchtime, on a Sunday. It's a social centre. There's no reason why a man shouldn't use it. But now you see men coming in, having to count the coppers. They're not denying the family anything by having a couple of pints. They put the family first. But whereas they would normally come and stand by four or five of you, they isolate themselves deliberately because they couldn't afford to get mixed up with other people. They haven't got the money. Their pride won't allow them to mix with other people. You don't go and stand with a man if you've got the price of two pints in your pocket and he's got the price to buy a round for the school that he's with. You're not going to go and stand with that school. And there's another awful blow to a man's pride.

'You get the sort of person who'll say, "Well, what's he doing in a pub anyway?" But then the question is, can you take a man's social life away from him completely? I mean, is it his fault he's redundant? Are you going to lock him up in his own little cell and say, "Well bad luck, until we can find you full employment again, social amenities are withdrawn from you – you don't smoke, you don't drink, if you've got a television, bad luck." This sort of thing. You ask me about pride and such like, this is where the pride bit comes. But of course this is a social problem. This isn't a British Leyland problem – this is a general problem throughout industry, throughout most aspects of life.'

Thus Bill describes a continuity, between the experience of work, the political response to that experience, and the problem of redundancy. The continuity is established in the whole context of his life; and particularly in how he defines himself – as a *man*. In our society the main focus of masculinity is the wage – 'providing', maintaining an emotional stability, and a place to 'relax'. It is the interpenetration of 'work' and 'home' that constitutes the taken-for-granted texture of working-class existence.

'I believe especially being a driver, you know, it's absolutely imperative that you relax completely when you've finished your job. You've got to be able to sit back and talk. I would say that I like to forget work when I'm away from work, since the two environments are so different. They don't mix. And let's be perfectly honest, the wife isn't interested in how you drive a wagon. Although I bring the wagon home occasionally and let the children have a sit in it and look at it. But I don't think the work environment and the home environment mix. I don't think you've a right to inflict your work on anybody else. Your work is a separate entity altogether – and when you're at home, home is home and that's it. Home is a place to relax, which brings us back to what I was saying – the need to relax when you're away from work. The man who brings his work home with him, who never stops working – you know the sort of feller I mean? You meet him socially, might be at a dance, and all he can talk about is his job and such like – I feel rather sorry for that man. He must have a very one-track life.

'The prime responsibility (of being a family man) is a stable life. By this I mean, incorporating clothing, food and the like, you know, maintaining a respectable standard of all those for your children, and having them love you. That's the biggest thing in a man's life – having your children love you. I mean, that's not sentimental. I have three nice children, and they're very proud of the job I do. My son is extremely proud, you know, "My Daddy drives a big lorry," and such like. In fact he's firmly convinced that when he grows up he's going to drive a big lorry. I'm equally firmly convinced that he's not going to! I'm very proud indeed that my children love me you know. And they do, I'm not boasting, they do. My son especially. I must confess that I spoil him a little. I want them to be happy.

'I'm not responsible for my work. I'm not responsible for the job I've got. I was led into that by circumstances, shall we say, as everybody is you know. But I am responsible for my family, since I am the prime source of their, well, being on earth. So therefore I must have a greater sense of responsibility towards them. I think every father must have. I mean, if one of my children were ill or anything like that, that child would come before anything. That's got to be, well that's just got to be a fact of life, hasn't it?'

Middle-class masculinity

To some extent, the lives of working and middle-class men are similarly structured. Both classes of men have inherited the patriarchal culture of the past and both experience the erosion of patriarchal privilege by capitalist expansion. Also most middle-class men pursue their masculinity in the conventional way: in an over-riding commitment to work, supported by an idealized image of 'home'. For most men, everyday life takes on a familiar structure: a daily routine of confrontation and challenge – followed by an evening's retirement to the family and relaxation. 'Domesticity' is the man's reward for performing his daily tasks.

But within this common cultural framework, middle-class masculinity has a distinctive character which is alien to the working class. There is a middle-class ideological world – the dominant, institutionalized code of behaviour and belief. This code supports an image of masculinity which the working-class man sees all around him – in the mass media, the courts of law, the education system, etc. – from which he cannot escape, and which in some respects (for it carries social status) he finds attractive. But it is an image which is, fundamentally, incongruent with his experience of the world. It is built around a notion of 'professionalism' – untenable, by definition, by the wage-labourer.

For the 'professional' differs from the 'worker' in two main respects. First, the middle-class professional does not do a 'job', he pursues a 'career'; he is paid not a 'wage', but a 'salary'; he works not by the 'clock', but by 'appointment'. His career is a long-term investment, a ladder of individual achievement, finally rewarded by the 'golden handshake'. The wage-labourer seeks at work a variety of jobs, and in good times he may voluntarily change his employment. But the 'professional' seeks promotion – which means cultivating a particular expertise, and of necessity being committed to the future. Middle-class work is less of a physical experience, performed in the company of others; more a lonely, inner struggle to achieve. The personal office, the telephone, the name-plate on the door, signify how far a man has come, and how far there is still to go.

Second, the 'professional ideal' is pervaded by a sense of moral justification, which is entirely absent from the world of wage-labour. Because the career is a long-term commitment, it requires a man's wholehearted identification. Typically, it demands a sense of 'duty', or 'obligation'. The discipline of middle-class work is not the impersonal discipline of factory production, but *self*-discipline, an internalized desire to work. This desire is sustained by a man's faith in an authority greater than himself: an Empire, the Nation, or at a local level, the 'community', 'civic pride'. His ethical code, and the 'self-respect' which it confers, is what drives a man towards greater and higher achievements. Raymond Williams provides a useful summary of this, the moral legacy of the traditional middle class:

> 'A very large part of English middle-class education is devoted to the training of servants. This is much more its characteristic than a training for leadership, as the stress on conformity and on respect for authority shows. In so far as it is by definition, the training of upper servants, it includes, of course, the instilling of that kind of confidence which will enable the upper servants to supervise and direct the lower servants. Order must be maintained there, by good management, and in this respect the function is not service but government. Yet the upper servant is not to think of his own interests. He must subordinate these to a larger good, which is called the Queen's peace, or national security, or law and order, or the public weal.'
>
> (Raymond Williams, 1958:329)

Together, the structure of the career and the ethic of service still dominate the working lives of most middle-class men. Even where the future is unpredictable, a working life is still seen as a

82

series of stages, leading finally to recognition by the community of individual achievement. It is an image of work open to few working-class men. For it requires the possession of *capital* : if not money for investment, then 'cultural capital' – an indispensible social expertise. It is his 'qualification' that gives the middle-class man the independence to direct his own future. It is because his 'qualification' is more than his own labour-power – being a special 'gift' which he employs for the benefit of others – that he is able to 'serve' an authority greater than himself.

Within the notion of 'professionalism' however, there are levels and distinctions, some of which touch the boundaries of the working-class world. The experience of professionalism differs with the type of work involved, and its relative status in the social hierarchy. At the top, the jet-propelled life-style of the industrial executive obviously differs from the conservative prestige of the army or the church. The snobbery of the solidly upper middle class has long been associated with a suspicion of 'trade' and 'bad taste'. Lower down the scale, in 'management' rather than 'administration', the overall ethical commitment to a career may be experienced more as routine obligation than a sense of privilege or pride. There are monotonous, thankless middle-class jobs as well as positions of power. Within the 'aristocracy' of the working class, certain attitudes towards 'skilled trades' are influenced by hegemonic middle-class definitions. The 'professional image' has entered occupations like the armed services (in their recruitment and training procedures) sports and entertainments (with their values of dedication and skill).

So it is difficult to make generalizations. In part, the world of middle-class work is highly differentiated, from the administrative and intellectual decision-makers, to 'white-collar' workers in clerical departments. It makes a substantial difference to his personal experience of work if a man can see the immediate effects of his decisions; if there are direct contacts with the community he serves; if he works alone or with others. But also, despite the specialization inherent in middle-class work, the 'professional ideal' as an ideology, has a unified history. And this history has traditionally involved a patriarchal definition of masculinity; which has been fundamentally undermined by developments in post-war capitalism.

The traditional professional identity was built upon an imperial image of masculine behaviour. Here, patriarchal tradition survived, not so much in local superstitions, as in a global network of international trade. A newly emergent class typically identifies with the prestigious culture of its predecessor; and the upper middle class in particular continued to define its economic power and to fight its imperial wars in terms of aristocratic ideas of 'manhood'. Originating in feudal conditions of patriarchal inheritance these ideas were expressed in a chivalric code – the masculine 'honour', bravado, and finesse, of the ideal courtier. In his public school the 'courtier' became the 'gentleman' – with an ideally balanced personality : personal honour tempered by duty to the crown.

As the Public School Commissioners put it themselves :

> 'It is not easy to estimate the degree in which the English people are indebted to these schools for the qualities on which they pique themselves most – for their capacity to govern others and control themselves, their aptitude for combining freedom with order, their public spirit, their vigour and manliness of character, their strong but not slavish respect for public opinion, their love of healthy sport and exercise. These schools have been the chief nurseries of our statesmen; in them, and in schools modelled after them, men of all the various classes that make up English society, destined for every profession and career, have been brought up on a footing of social equality, and have contracted the most enduring friendships, and some of the ruling habits of their lives; and they have had perhaps the largest share in moulding the character of an English Gentleman.'

(Kitson Clark, 1962 : 271)

As I have already described, the 'vigour and manliness' of a public-school education was typically internalized in an obsessive masculinity. At the expense of his finer feelings, a boy learned to avoid the expression of emotion, and to devote himself to a hierarchy of achievement. Fed by fantasies of sexual

84

mastery, his fragile ego was bound by a need for recognition. His personality was ideally placed for a professional career – a lifetime's struggle for success and reward.

When I left home and entered university, my feelings were a mixture of excitement and trepidation. A determination to succeed was coupled with a fear of others – that they were better prepared, less provincial, than I. The men, at first seemed sure of themselves; the women, vivacious and socially graceful. In classes I was quiet and watchful; but as my confidence grew I began to speak, as coherently as I could, making what I hoped were useful contributions to the common intellectual 'debate'. I thought the situation should be an 'exchange of ideas', and I learned that the common form of exchange was between recognizable 'points of view' – the Religious, the Marxist, the Humanist, the Liberal, etc. You opened your mouth to indicate 'where you stood': 'It seems to me, from my position that ...'; 'The point I want to make is this ...'; and so on.

It became more and more apparent to me that this exchange was conducted mainly between the men. The women on the course became silent – a fact which was easily attributed to their 'lack of interest'. They were, after all, only there to 'find a husband'. I, on the other hand, was now part of a masculine debate – expected to voice my opinions and to conduct formal arguments with my opponents. Is Hamlet, a renaissance prince, representative of the declining, feudal aristocracy or the emerging bourgeoisie? Or are such criteria relevant at all to what is, after all, an esthetic masterpiece? The discussion was stage-managed for stock contributions, the making of 'points', or ironic jokes at the expense of others. It was the classic intellectual 'forum'; the market-place of ideas.

Still the erstwhile vivacious women remained strangely silent. At times I suppose I felt the silence directed at me. I felt my speeches to be self-parodies, and in my public persona I began to cultivate a certain cynicism. I could always, as a last resort, bluff my way out of an opponent's manoeuvres by tactics such as 'name-dropping' (quoting 'authorities' you have never read) or picking on the trivial points in arguments. This was the thrill of a kind of intellectual poker, where the carefully concealed ace caps the argument. As the exams approached, my friend (a man) had a nervous breakdown. My flat-mate took to drinking himself to sleep. I determinedly set out to prove I could make it; systematically tailored my thoughts to suit the possible questions.

This 'liberal education' is a professional game: it has complex rules which transform an involvement with people and books into strategies for individual success (or failure). It is a game most men cannot resist, because it can be dealt with through the masculine personality developed at school, and because it is continually supported by dominant images of power and reward. No 'real man' shies away from a challenge. But in the midst of his manoeuvres it is often difficult for him to see what is happening. Only in retrospect does he begin to realize that the 'open forum' is closed; that the 'points of view' are stereotypes. In the masculine world there is no room for introspection. He who cracks up fails his exams: it is as simple, and brutal, as that.

Thus, by the time a middle-class man enters his 'chosen profession', work has become self-confirming. The career-structure reinforces his expectations, and stimulates a particular set of conditioned responses. It is impossible to isolate the moment when this kind of behaviour is 'learned'. It is a whole process of socialization: picking up the signals, reading the intentions and weaknesses of others, making the appropriate 'interventions'. In the upper middle classes, this kind of social interaction is still mediated by the 'stiff-upper-lip' of the 'English gentleman'; who remains limited by an inability to open-up, to express his doubts, and, as I experienced at university, by an insensitivity to what is really going on.

In contemporary Britain, however, and in particular echelons of the social hierarchy, there has developed what I shall describe as a professional 'crisis of confidence'. A substantial historical shift in the circumstances of some middle-class men has shaken the professional ethic to its foundations – and a split within the traditional masculine identity seems to be beginning to emerge. In part, the post-war reconstruction of British society has stripped away the idealistic cloak surrounding middle-class work and has revealed, for the first time, its naked insecurity.

More and more men have begun to see the career-structure as futile, and impossible to sustain. But also, the 'crisis of confidence' has undermined that notion of 'teamwork' which, in the wake of 'duty' to the Empire, the modern business corporation has tried to develop. With no ethical commitment to the institution he serves, the middle-class man comes face-to-face with his motivation to work at all.

The internal structure of the career always had an inbuilt insecurity. It was a hierarchy of personal achievement where each attained position was threatened by competition from below. There was a fear of losing control, not of external forces, but of personal power and indispensability. A fear of incompetence nagged the executive – not a social alienation from another's control, but a fear of self-destruction. The anguish of the decision-maker was the perpetual worry, not that he had made the wrong decision, but that he would be unable to make decisions at all. But as long as he could accept the higher goals of the enterprise – the 'put-downs' and the personal insecurity of competition could be justified by simply 'doing his best' with dedication and humility.

However, with the development of post-war capitalism, middle-class managerial functions have expanded and diversified. It has been an age of 'meritocracy', especially within the bureaucracies of industrial corporations and within the apparatus of the State. The diversification of company investments, the sophistication of technological processes, the growth of plant administration (especially production control) has demanded technical planning at the point of production. The development of servicing industries, transport, mass-communications, and advertising, has created opportunities in distribution and exchange. Simultaneously, as this 'managerial revolution' has developed, its ideological foundation has declined. The withering away of Britain's international power, and subsequently in the 'seventies, the demise of the British economy itself, have together destroyed the credibility of the professional ideal. Beyond its intrinsic satisfactions (an internal dynamic of personal advancement) the modern, bureaucratic career lacks any moral justification, and where the moral authority is undermined, 'duty' and 'self-discipline' lack recognizable meaning.

As I discuss middle-class masculinity, the dimensions of this post-war 'crisis of confidence' will, I hope, become clearer. At work, the crisis has been met, in typically masculine fashion, by a withdrawal into cynicism covering up a sense of disillusionment. Nowhere is this response more apparent than in the teaching profession; which, in a society where so many working-class and immigrant children reject the middle-class culture of their teachers, is fundamentally demoralized by a collapse of educational ideals. Today's teacher lives out directly, in the classroom, the ideological contradictions of a decaying imperialist, class-ridden society. He sees his life as a game of chess, in which he is the player, but also, if he is honest, the pawn:

'Everybody watches everybody else. It's like a cat stalking a mouse. You see, there's very few opportunities, and you watch everybody else. It's like "The Power Game" on the telly, if you remember that. You know, where they used to sit in the boardroom and discuss all these matters. Well I feel like that in a way; only the boardroom's my brain, you know, and I sort of think out all the different ways and means of how I can manoeuvre myself into the best position. It's like a giant game of chess, you know: how can I get to there, so that I can eventually get to there? But I've got to be able to leave myself open to move over there if I need to. It's quite interesting really, sort of juggling around with yourself. And you're still waiting for the other person to make the move because you can't move until he's moved. This is the thing. And as soon as he's moved you've got to move in quick.'

In the 'white-hot' world of corporate industry, ideological cynicism is reflected in the expression of masculinity at work. The collective interaction of men working together is conducted from a distance; it is a formal advertisement for male solidarity in an essentially false situation. When they are together, where a collective atmosphere shields an individual's restraint, male clerical workers will draw attention to swearing, make an issue of a woman entering the office, watch her suggestively as she passes by. In the soft-pornography which they exchange, their masculine aspirations are capitalized by the image of the 'playboy' – fast cars, sharp suits, glamorous 'birds'. They will dress up to attend city-centre night clubs with their wives, becoming, however tentatively, a 'swinging couple'. Together with the women in the office, men will make (in Birmingham at least) 'wedding books' to celebrate colleagues' marriages. These are often witty, sometimes crude, collections of sexual innuendos cut out from trade journals and magazines, stuck together in suggestive juxtaposition, tied up with ribbon, and presented to the happy couple. As one office worker in a large Birmingham factory observed:

'There's quite a sort of embarrassing interchange really. I mean the guys who I work with are quite shy in presenting what they've done, 'cause they're very crude and blatant. It has to be slipped in quickly, and then watched from a distance to see what the response is. But you can't actually talk about things like the existence of sex in a face-to-face confrontation. 'Cause that would be too embarrassing.'

As he moves up the career hierarchy, the sexual embarrassment of the middle-class man takes on a more serious implication. For a man's preoccupation with his own promotion often includes an explicit demand for sexual recognition. The high-flying executive begins to need the female colleague to let him know that he is 'doing OK': he needs to be 'mothered' through confrontations and disappointments. In this, the 'new managerialism', the professional's obsession with images of women has become a systematic psychological dependence. The 'girl' in his office works to symbolize his success. Her own prospects, and day-to-day behaviour are the necessary extension of his achievement.

A friend in the Women's Liberation Movement described to me her relationship to her boss:

'It's not so much your actual status; it's the way that you're treated in situations which is much more subtle and more difficult. You know that you're not actually regarded as a person. I know that's simplified, but men see you as a woman first and whatever position you are second ... They don't like intelligent women, that's the main thing, or women who are capable. 'Cause it's very undermining you know. Men find me threatening. I mean usually you're in a slightly inferior position to a man. His ego is constantly threatened, is constantly in a very dodgy state. And any sign of competence on my part is totally undermining of him, you know. What I have to do is not appear to be competent. To make it appear that he's making the decisions and that he's having the ideas, and to be supportive, to sort of boost him along so that he can do things. I think that men find women in Women's Liberation very threatening because they assume that if you're in Women's Liberation therefore you're promiscuous, therefore you are very much of a sexual threat to them. They know they can't dominate you very easily.'

A young middle-class man still approaches his career with excitement, for it is his personal destiny, and will fix his social identity. For the rest of his life he will be asked the routine cocktail-party questions: 'What line are you in?'; 'What do you do?' He will be categorized and dealt with on the impression of his answer. But in an increasingly bureaucratic society, his experience of work slowly compromises a man's heroic visions. In the face of administrative drudgery, machiavellian dealings and cut-throat competition (not only for business contracts but also for recognition and praise) he develops a 'business personality', a front, a combination of detachment and uncertainty. His decisions make the system work, but he is not responsible for its workings. If he allows himself to be at all sensitive to the often frustrating decisions he has to make (destroying neighbourhoods in the name of redevelopment; making colleagues redundant in the name of efficiency), his apparent self-confidence will be backed up by serious moral doubts. Typically, however, his irony on the one hand, and moral posture on the other, are both over-ridden by an old middle-class mythology of work; an unquestioning commitment, wrestling with problems, attending minutely to details. Despite his doubts and torments, the work-ethic, with its 'kick' of self-discipline, it's 'high' of delayed gratification, must serve to justify itself.

Of course, the tendency I am describing here is general, and has an uneven development. It is more likely to be felt in large bureaucracies and corporations, rather than small family firms. It is more a feature of metropolitan societies, than provincial towns. But the professional 'crisis of confidence' is widespread enough for two classic masculine responses to be identified. First, as I have already illustrated, the individual is frequently thrown back upon himself, into his career, which now becomes a matter for overtly cynical calculation. And second, to which I now turn, the disillusioned professional is forced, with new impetus, back to the focus of all his patriarchal attitudes : the home, and the family.

The demands placed upon the family by men reflect the nature of their alienation from work. As we have seen, the working-class man's attitude to his 'leisure' is a reflex from the drudgery of the factory; and for the wage-labourer, it is the symbolic culmination of his 'freedom'. But the alienation of middle-class men, being due less to direct exploitation and more to complex ideological contradictions, is *psychological* in character. It is, as I have described, a crisis of personal *identification*. The patriarchal attitudes a man brings home are mediated by moral doubts, and demands for emotional sustenance. His 'leisure' is not so much a search for 'free time', for 'peace and quiet', as for an intimate, and fulfilling quality of relationships.

In the middle-class world the division between 'work' and 'home' is flexible. Unlike the manual worker, the professional will bring his work home, and involve his wife in his daily problems — especially the personality conflicts of office life. Concerned how he relates, as a father, to his children, he will participate in their play, involve himself in their education, and demand, in return, that they respect him. Above all, throughout the middle-class world, great emphasis is placed upon the *ethic* of family life itself — what the family stands for, the myth of 'domesticity'. Here, the family as such is idealized as the centre of discipline and 'respectability'. It is not only at the centre of 'leisure', but also at the hub of 'civilization' — the 'decent' society which, to the professional middle class, is seemingly losing its stature and foundation.

Traditionally an idea of 'home' has always been one of the key components of British imperialism. For men, this idea was sufficiently flexible to refer both to the immediate nuclear family – the psychological focus of 'manhood'; and to the community, or the nation – the ideological focus of the English 'gentleman'. Particularly in the imperialist wars, soldiers fought for women and children 'back home': being 'one of the boys' in the armed services was to reaffirm the inevitability and the righteousness of warfare. With the war-effort, the whole nation became 'one big family'. Here for example, Bert Fielder, a professional soldier in the Royal Marines, writes home during the First World War:

'I should like it to finish tomorrow but I should like it to finish properly, that is that Germany gets such a smashing that she won't be able to try the experiment again for a good many years, not during our lifetime or our Boy's life-time, you see it's no use to indulge in selfish thoughts, that is thinking of your own happiness, we are not only fighting for our present happiness, but fighting for the generation that is to come into the world, which takes our place when we are gone, these little ones will never forget us when they grow up, when they read in history of these terrible times when their fathers were fighting and their mothers were living in terrible agony in the old home, oh yes, let it go on, until this race of Evil Human Demons are wiped off the face of God's earth.'

(Michael Moynihan, 1975 : 51)

The sustaining ideal of 'the old home' gave a man his place in history, and a moral justification for fighting in the war. But it is significant that his most abstract thoughts, are interwoven with memories of his son, and 'my little grey home in the West':

'Always you are both in my thoughts, I think of you both in that little kitchen by yourselves and know that you are think-ing of me and wondering perhaps if you will ever see me come back again, every night at nine o'clock out here which is seven o'clock in England, I think that it is the Boy's bed-time and I always can picture him kneeling in his cot saying his prayers after Mummy. But "Cheer up", my Scrumps, this will all end soon and we shall be together again and carry on the old life once more.

'My dear Scrumps, I wonder if the Boy still thinks of the gun I promised to bring home ... So his latest craze is fishing is it, yes I'm afraid I'm missing a lot of his amusing little ways, but I shall make up for it when I get home, oh that glorious time when the boys *do* get home. But I shall always be pleased to read any accounts you can send me of him, as I fancy I'm at home when I read about him.'

(Michael Moynihan, 1975 : 47, 53)

If the patriarchal sentiment of the working-class man was expressed in a nostalgia for 'home sweet home', the equivalent middle-class attitude was a picture of 'domestic bliss'. Here, the right moral standards were expressed by 'manners', and by shows of affection, which formally respected the authority of the father-figure. Surrounded by his dependants, a middle-class man felt his moral dignity confirmed. His personal commitment to a career was supported by the notion that he was 'being a good father'. His righteous moralism entered into his most particular daily interactions defining the 'standards' that he set for the family as a whole. And the extent of this authority was confirmed by the 'double standard' which he often reserved for himself.

Today, it is in the provincial, lower middle class that these 'bourgeois' attitudes survive. A self-employed builder and decorator, struggling successfully to build up his own business, described to me the interaction in his life between 'work' and 'home'. He could not avoid long hours and financial worries, and he apologized for the sacrifices his family had to make. He was distinctly uncertain whether he was a 'good father', but the knowledge that he was respected for his work compensated for the doubts. He went on to elaborate how the 'respect' of his family showed itself in personal relationships :

'If I was to be lazy, I wouldn't feel good. I wouldn't feel right. It's just in my nature. Actually I think I should feel ashamed of myself if I couldn't put a day's work in for anybody else, or for myself. I'd feel I was letting myself down. And it leads to letting the family down as well. You see the

93

family think the world of you; and you go and do things like that, and you're betraying their trust. That's how I think.

'In as much as I get work right, and do that right, then the family's all right. I'd have to say it in that order. If I can't do my work well, then I'm no good to myself, and then in turn I'm no good to them, you know. It involves money obviously. I mean that's why we go out to work most often. And then I think you lose some of your dignity if you haven't got the right amount of money. But I think I can do a job well, and that makes me good, makes me feel good, to know that I can do it well. If I even was a roadsweeper and I did that well, I'd still be as good a father as I think I am now. Someone they can respect. I've got to give them something to respect. I want them to have someone to look up to.

'And I know they respect me 'cause they love me. And they show their love you see. It isn't just a flippant kiss on the cheek, there's some feeling in it. There's no falseness there – well, I wouldn't stand that anyway. If it became false then I'd have to have it out with them. What's gone wrong? Who's gone wrong? You know. I mean we do sort things out. Not this respect business, but there are different things. If they have a long face you know, if they're sulking or anything, I've got to get to the bottom of it. And they've never sulked for long. Because I've always told them, you know, I won't stand it. This is when I get on my high horse: "We'll have no sulking in this house." And they don't sulk for long. I probably sulk for longer than they do – but then, I'm allowed to ...'[2]

The self-analysis of the 'family man' gives the middle-class family its distinctive ideological character. For the introspection does not necessarily indicate a superior quality of family relationships; what it points to is a *desire* that these relationships be seen to be superior, or at least, 'respectable'. The authoritative tone of the father, carried through tales of the war, travels, and work, filters into the world-view of the child. Reinforced by the drama of filial affection, this perpetuates a dominant, masculine version of social reality: a man who does not work well is no good to himself, and no good to the family that has placed its trust in him.

For the disillusioned male careerist, this myth of 'domesticity' has become his last remaining source of support. Against the anxiety of his professional 'crisis of confidence' he will still make domestic plans, direct operations, project himself into the future. As husband and father, he is the *subject* of an ideology to which his wife and children are the *objects* – of his concern, his protection, his authority. And his focal position is maintained by a continuing *economic* power – the material reality to which the ideology corresponds.

But to the extent that his professional 'self' is undermined, a man's position within the home itself becomes a destructive force. Typically, the demoralized professional projects a domestic 'haven' – in which he seeks, from his dependents an appreciative and understanding audience. The reality of the domestic situation often gets confused with an imperative – that this is how things *ought* to be; and institutionalized shows of affection become the only currency for family relationships. In the modern middle-class family there are three particular points of stress, which I shall here describe in turn: the relationship of the married couple; interactions between parents and children; and the definitions given to sexuality. In each of these areas, because of his insecurity, but also because the myth of 'domesticity' legitimates his patriarchal presence, the middle-class 'family man' determines the suffering of others.

The relationship of the middle-class couple has always been weighted by the moralism of the masculine presence. This moralism shows itself in the attitude of superiority assumed by the husband; a prerogative of knowledge (he has all the answers), and thus a premium on judgement and decision-making. Of course the wife has some authority within her own sphere: care of the children and the home. But it is her husband who defines the limits of this sphere; and in so far as the life of the family encounters the outside world, then he is expected to project a kind of all-knowing, protective concern. Ideally, it is he who chooses the couple's social activities; he who selects acquaintances and friends. And because he cannot admit to ignorance, he covers up with endless rationalizations.

The following transcript of a taped dialogue illustrates very well the traditional structure of the lower middle-class couple. In this case, the family lives in a newly-built, high-rise block of council flats. The wife, Jean, who has working-class origins, finds that the pressure of home life, children, and the complaints of a neighbour 'gets on her nerves'. The husband, Ted, an aspiring production manager in an engineering factory, tries to sympathize by offering explanations:

Jean: 'He complained, and on the Friday that he did complain he said to me, he said, "Oh you went out this afternoon for ten minutes didn't you?" and I said, "Yes, why, how do you know?" and he said, "Oh I know what time you go out and what time you come in." '

Ted: 'Well with these big windows darling it's obvious that he knows what time you go out and what time you come in.'

Jean: 'Yes, I know but . . .'

Ted: 'You see, he's a retired gentleman and I think it . . .'

Jean: 'Gentleman? It's not what I call him.'

Ted: 'I think it's probably boredom.'

Jean: 'He's got nothing to do all day. He said he's in the house all day, and all he does is gets a paper and reads a paper. So he's just sitting there. Well I mean I've got jobs to do, and in and out to the children. But the noise he probably heard was first thing in the morning when I'm getting them ready for school. You know what it's like – getting the two of them washed and dressed, myself washed and dressed; and you know, like at breakfast they might be having a game with something, and I do sometimes shout at them you know. I say, "Come on, hurry up, you'll be late for school," and "Hurry up and finish your breakfast," and he can probably hear that, but you've got to live haven't you?'

Ted: 'Well, you see it's a free country darling, and the gentleman's got a perfect right to complain. Whether you take action on his complaint is up to you. He's a perfect right to complain.'

Jean: 'I know. But it's just, I can't do anything about it you know. If I was the sort of person who let the children come round on their bikes or have a ball, then I could understand his complaining. But he's only complaining he can hear footsteps you know. And he says if you drop anything, he can hear that.'

Ted: 'I think it's probably having so much time on his own, these things ... I mean, if you are sitting there doing nothing, then every little sound to you is magnified.'

Jean: 'Oh yes, I understand that but ...'

Ted: 'Whereas if he was a chappie that was sort of, doing something all the while, building or making something you know, or a younger family, they probably wouldn't notice it.'

Jean: 'Well, I mean all these sort of things, you know, well, it really worried me because I'm on edge all the time. As soon as Adam comes in from school I say, "Take your shoes off." And then he'll be on the floor perhaps, playing marbles, and I'll say, "Don't bang." And I'm saying this, I bet you I could say it three hundred times a day : "Don't bang, don't get on your knees, don't walk heavy on the floor." '

Ted: 'But you mustn't let it get you like that.'

Jean: 'And it does, it gets me all tense like ...'

Ted: 'I say you mustn't let it get you like that.'

Jean: 'I can't help it. Like tonight, when he came in, I was really on edge you know.'

Ted: 'Yes you were in a right tizwaz tonight.'

Jean: 'I was, you know, like 'cause the girl came round from next door. I didn't mind her coming round. But you know when all the children ... Well, there was my two and her young lad, and they was only playing, but I was thinking, "Oh he can hear them though." '

Ted: 'Yes, but you see, you mustn't let yourself get like that, darling. Otherwise you will take it out on the children.'

Jean: 'I do.'

Ted: 'Yes, well this is wrong.'

The outcome of this exchange is predictable. Ted's concern moves through his offering 'constructive theories' ('I think it's probably boredom'), to ideological platitudes ('It's a free coun-

97

try, darling'), and patronizing advice ('You mustn't let yourself get like that'). The condescension implicit in the advice fails to tackle the real problem – at its root a combination of inadequate housing, and a restrictive division of labour. It simply reproduces as her guilt and anxiety, the wife's isolation. In this way the structure of the couple supports the status quo. It is a fundamentally conservative institution, counselling adjustment and acceptance rather than radical social change. Through the power of the husband, the wife is trapped – and the myth of 'domesticity' justifies, even idealizes, her personal unhappiness.

The conservative character of the middle-class family is also enshrined in the ways parents treat children. Dependent upon parental provision, children are also trapped in the domestic world. In the traditional home, as we have seen, two attitudes especially are demanded: 'respect' for elders, and 'love' or 'affection'. A father requires that his superior status be upheld, and that the value of his career be recognized. So the development of children is channelled towards father's projection of himself. There is a complex psychological interaction between the 'outside world' in which father is involved, the demands for filial respect which he brings home, and the growth of a child's own personality. A great deal depends, for the middle-class child, on whether the world opened up by father's professional career, is successful and secure.

Because an element of insecurity is built into the structure of the middle-class career, a middle-class man will often introduce a certain compulsion into his relationships with his children. Children are forced to live out the projects of fathers who have 'invested', financially and emotionally, in their futures. To make independent decisions is to confront the power of paternal accusation: 'After all I've done for you ...'; 'I've given you everything I never had ...' Some of the famous case studies of R. D. Laing (though Laing's own theoretical bias leads to an emphasis on maternal rather than paternal anxiety) illustrate the extremely problematic consequences of the father's traditional role:

'The uncle thought that though the father was very fond of the boy in his way, something seemed to stop him from being able

98

to show his affection to him. He tended to be gruff, to pick on faults, occasionally to thrash him for no good reason, and to belittle him with such remarks as "Useless Eustace," "You're just a big lump of dough." The uncle thought that this was a pity because when he did well at school and later got a job in an office, which was a big step up socially for this very poor family, he really was "terribly proud of that boy"; it was "a terrible blow to him" when his son seemed later just not to want to make anything of himself ... In the Army, at his own wish, he looked after patrol dogs and when he left, after serving two years without incident, he "broke his father's heart" by, literally, "going to the dogs", in that he obtained a job as a kennelman at a dog track. He left this, however, after a year, and after five months doing various unskilled jobs he simply did nothing for seven months before he went to his general practitioner complaining of smell.'

(R. D. Laing, 1960:131-2)

Peter's symptoms point not merely to a psychological disorder, but also to a deeply ambivalent family environment. The authority of the father demands the obedience of the son. But the son is simultaneously expected to 'stand on his own two feet', 'to make something of himself'. The syndrome is crystallized in Freud's theory of the 'Oedipus Complex': the son identifies with the father's masculinity – but fears the power of his authority ('Wait till your father gets home'). But Freud's theory, by retreating to Greek mythology for an explanation, fails to comprehend the social context of the Oedipus Complex. It is a psychological ambivalence consequent upon the father's position within the bourgeois family. Paternal 'affection' is filtered through 'respect'; communication takes place at a distance; tenderness is framed by bourgeois moralism. A father jokingly plays the wolf with his son, and threatens to 'gobble him up', weaving fearful fantasies of castration in the boy's mind. A growing boy is unable to trust his own feelings; he is pulled in two directions by a 'double-bind' he cannot escape.

In times of social change, the psychological ambivalence of the Oedipus Complex intersects the shifting of social relationships. Sons become unrecognizable to their fathers – as they adopt new life-styles, or assume independent social identities. This, the 'generation gap', is no inevitable rejection of paternal affection; but it is experienced as such within the traditional middle-class family. Because of the patriarchal affinity between fathers and sons – ideological contradictions are taken personally. Filial rivalry becomes a relationship of open hostility, where claims and counter-claims take on their own momentum, further and further away from the centre of the problem. The disillusioned father, caught inside a web of communications he cannot control, is forced into an aggressive dogmatism. The guilt-ridden son, acting out his rebellion with increasing petulance, is reduced to a cynical self-parody.

A third point of domestic stress, at the centre of all family life, is the monogamous sexual relationship. The quest for sexual fulfilment has always been a major theme of middle-class culture – in literature, and in private fantasies of mystery and romance. But in the old bourgeois family a tightly-woven pattern of propriety and euphemism drove this mystery underground. Sexual recognition was locked into an armour of 'respectability'. Predetermined by an ambivalent relationship with his father, a man's sexual awakening took place either in a home dominated by women (mothers, sisters, nurses, servants) or in the exclusively-male public school. The atmosphere of constraint was almost tangible – embarrassed blushes, and smiles – the stuff of bourgeois novelists.

Such repression has meant that middle-class sexuality, both for men and for women, has had the character of a quest. A sort of dialectic is set up between repression and fulfilment, so that each dynamically feeds off the other. There is a qualitative difference between the non-exclusive 'friendship', and the special experience of 'falling in love', for which sexual fulfilment is reserved. In the supreme moment the forces of repression are felt to coalesce, in spontaneous feelings bestowed upon another 'unique' individual. Such feelings remain unanalysed; one feels what one is supposed to feel. And sex is, above all, a *private* experience: erotic desires are lonely, silent, undiscussed.

For men, the ambiguities of middle-class sexuality typically combine in the most pervasive of double-binds. A man seeks, not one woman, but two: the 'angel' and the 'femme fatale'. On the one hand, social propriety leads to marriage and responsibilities. On the other hand, the romantic imagination paints pictures of excitement and seduction. The 'angel' is characteristically sympathetic, domestic, modest-looking. The 'femme fatale' is unpredictable, tempting, and looks you in the eye. One becomes your wife, the object of 'affection'; the other is the mistress of 'desire'.

D. H. Lawrence has been quoted by feminist writers as the apotheosis of patriarchal sexuality. But in bourgeois terms, and from the man's point of view, his achievement was radical – for he attempted to bring the two sides of the masculine fantasy together. Lawrence made a virtue of repressed romanticism. Emotional distance now became 'otherness'; a recognition of an essential space between free individuals. In *Women In Love*, Birkin formulates, in a classic passage, the central paradox of Lawrence's philosophy – that intensely moral amorality which captivated the 'free-thinkers' of the last generation:

' "There is," he said, in a voice of pure abstraction, "a final me which is stark and impersonal and beyond responsibility. So there is a final you. And it is there I would want to meet you – not in the emotional, loving plane – but there beyond, where there is no speech and no terms of agreement. There we are two stark, unknown beings, two utterly strange creatures, I would want to approach you, and you me. And there could be no obligation, because there is no standard for action there, because no understanding has been reaped from that plane. It is quite inhuman – so there can be no calling to book, in any form whatsoever – because one is outside the pale of all that is accepted, and nothing known applies. One can only follow the impulse, taking that which lies in front, and responsible for nothing, asked for nothing, giving nothing, only each taking according to the primal desire."

'Ursula listened to this speech, her mind dumb and almost senseless, what he said was so unexpected and so untoward.

' "It is just purely selfish," she said.

' "If it is pure, yes. But it isn't selfish at all. Because I don't *know* what I want of you. I deliver *myself* over to the unknown, in coming to you, I am without reserves or defences, stripped entirely, into the unknown. Only there needs the pledge between us, that we will both cast off everything, cast off ourselves even, and cease to be, so that that which is perfectly ourselves can take place in us." '

(D. H. Lawrence, 1954:137–8)

Increasingly disillusioned with his professional ideal, sex becomes the essential moment of a man's self-assertion. But the one-sided nature of his assertion is illustrated, in the above dialogue, by the character of Ursula – 'dumb', 'senseless', passive. Like every other aspect of the life of the couple, sexual passion is defined in *masculine* terms. Men give, women accept; men initiate, women 'respond' – extending male dominance into the sexual relationship itself. From a woman's point of view, her sexuality is doubly repressed: both by the constraints of the home, and by the self-assertions of insecure men. It is significant that in *Women In Love* the Laurentian 'sexual revolution' amounts to a sleight of hand: the partnership of Ursula and Birkin is paralleled by the mutual destruction of Gudrun and Gerald. Gudrun's independence, because it challenges the privilege and dominance of the man, is precisely what middle-class sexuality finds impossible to incorporate. Birkin's fine speeches are thus made at Gudrun's expense; and Lawrence has retreated to two images of women.

Alan is a teacher in a comprehensive school in a northern industrial town. He is recently married, to another teacher with a child from a previous marriage. In his description of his life, Alan particularly emphasizes the constant, inter-penetration of his career and family life. He considers very carefully his financial pressures, his career options, and the dream of a future 'home of our own'. 'Home' is one of the careerist's calculations – a place for homework and long-term planning. But also, as he himself is increasingly aware, 'home' represents a compensation for the often frustrating routine of the classroom. It is, as Alan puts it, a 'taken-for-granted' world of mutual 'give-and-take'.

As a young teacher, in his second post, Alan is forced to confront the realities of his 'chosen career'. He is quite explicit, that the values of 'dedication' and 'commitment' still supposedly attached to the teaching profession, are, in his view, a source of exploitation. As the economic measure of personal 'worth', the salary is the basic material calculation:

'I reckon I'm worth twice as much as I get. And that's not an exaggeration, the amount of work I put in. You see if I was to take my salary as a forty-hour week – that's just the school time – I'm paid at – I think I worked it out – that it was 65p an hour. Well, I reckon that's just appearance money as far as I'm concerned. I mean, that doesn't account for the whole day on Sunday that I spend preparing lessons; the Tuesday, Wednesday nights that I usually spend marking books. It doesn't take into account that I spent four hours this week refereeing rugby matches. I mean it must bring my average pay down to what – twenty or thirty pence an hour. Well, I was getting that when I was sixteen! You know, they say that teaching's a vocation, but if they want a good job done and they want to attract teachers into the job, they're going to have to start looking to get some money. I mean, if a miner's worth sixty quid a week to go down hewing coal, they ought to think about paying the teachers sixty quid a week to educate them.

'I mean, I look at it this way, I've got a life to lead. I've got my family, and I don't want to be left with a mortgage of ninety-odd pound a month, and things like this, till I'm sixty-five. Meaning that we've both got to keep on working till the bitter end. I don't see why I should stop in teaching when I can go down the steelworks, and work nine till four, for more than twice the salary. Whereas I'm working all hours God sends at the moment. The only thing I'm seriously thinking of is the fact that as I get older, you know, that six-week holiday is going to mean a hell of a lot. And I'm sort of weighing up, do I want the holidays, and the relatively easy life once you get yourself established in a school, and the kids know you, and they know what they can do and what they can't do – then you know your life is relatively easy. And this peace of mind I think is worth a hell of a lot of money.'

Dissatisfaction with the rewards of teaching, is supported by a growing disillusionment with the organization of school. Like many professionals, the teacher is part of 'front-line' management – his personality is the focus of an immediate contradiction between 'authority' and 'disobedience'. As Alan describes, he is obliged to develop strategies of control: 'It's very much an act, more than anything else.' Behind the formal gamesmanship persists a feeling for the kids; but attention can only be shown to individuals, in the form of personal counselling. In the vast, impersonal context of the comprehensive school, even 'pastoral care' is a specialized avenue of promotion:

'The kids themselves are nice enough. They work reasonably well, you don't push them all the time. O-level kids now, it's mainly me, standing at the front, lecturing, them taking notes. They do a couple of exercises, draw a map, answer questions, write essays. CSE, that's where you start pulling the tricks out of the book you know, looking at your approach to get over virtually the same material that you had at O-level, but making it interesting. So you end up with the same end-product, but how you've achieved those ends is totally different. Remedial, I use a lot of project work with them. I just mainly occupy them in geography and try to make them appreciate that it's not just an academic subject, take newspaper clippings and things like this in, to make it as topical as I possibly can. I know what I'm doing with the remedial class, and I don't spend much time preparing lessons for them.

'I tend to use the maps out of text books, but I put these on to an overhead projector, because then they're looking at me, I'm the central focal point, I've got their attention. You know, you're there and they're all looking at you pointing, and the screen's up behind you, you see. You're looking and talking at the kids, and you can see who isn't paying attention, and who's going to sleep, and this sort of thing. And you've got much more control than if you're just saying, "Look at your text books, page forty-eight." I don't do that at all.

'And I find that I don't have any trouble. I work at getting a reputation, so if the kids come up to me, into my lesson, or when I walk into a substitution, they know they're not going to get away with anything. If I get my discipline in the first half-term of a year, it makes life really tolerable for the rest of the year. With remedial kids it's easy. You know they won't step out of line. But then I've got a class which is not quite remedial – but one stage above remedial – and with them I entertain. And that lesson I really earn the money because the kids are bright enough to play up, and they're not bright enough to accept the standards that you really want them to have. It's very much an act, more than anything else. I really want to get them interested, because I don't think school should be just purely and simply for learning a set of facts. I want to interest them in other parts of the world – different customs, different ideologies. Where it's not just plain straightforward fact-taking – when it's not O-level – I can interest kids. But I find it difficult to interest kids on an O-level syllabus. It's the same work for two years.

'I'm on two or three committees. I'm a form teacher, therefore you're helping the admin. of the school you know, the pastoral side of it. But mainly the administration is not done by the common-or-garden teacher – it's done by the Head, the Deputy Head, the Headmistress, you know, these type of people. All you come across is when you're supplying them with information about certain kids. It's not as organized as it possibly could be. We play at it more than anything else in this school. I think you've got to work as a team, looking into problems. If a kid's got a problem, talk to him about it if he wants to talk about it – if he doesn't want to talk about it, leave him alone. But watch him. These are the sorts of things that have got to be done. I resent not being paid for working. That's the biggest thing. I don't mind working, but to be perfectly frank I'm in teaching not because I particularly like it – although I do enjoy the job – but the qualifications I got didn't leave me much option of what I was going to do. Even though I wanted to be a teacher. I think if I'd gone to university, I don't think I'd have ended up in teaching. I probably would have ended up in something completely different. But I mean, fair enough, it's what I've ended up as – I'm quite happy in my job. It's rewarding. If I get the promotion I want, I'll stick with it. Because if I get the promotion that I want it will leave me in a very strong position to be into the big money in teaching. You see, if I'm a Head of Department, or a Head of School by the time I'm thirty, thirty-five, I'm in line for a Deputy Headship by the time I'm forty. Well, I mean, I'm all right then, I'm laughing.'

In his life as a whole, Alan's professional calculations are 'balanced' by two principle interests: sport and his family. The weekly game of rugby provides a symbolic escape from teaching – a knife-edge of physical sublimation on which the professional routine depends. Here, the explicit masculinity of the game itself – a mixture of mock heroism and camaraderie – provides a kind of regression back to the world of 'the boys'. But at home, relaxation is part of the professional responsibility – marking, preparing lessons. As Alan indicates, domestic life is rationed as the sense of 'duty' prevails:

'When we go out together we always go to the rugby club for a drink. We always start off there, or we end up there. But the rugby club is the centre, certainly of my social life. And in a large respect it is Val's as well, because Val doesn't go out much, but when she does go out she always goes with me, and as such we always tend to go to the rugby club. When I give up playing rugby I shall still go to the rugby club. But as far as I'm concerned, the main reason for the rugby club is so I can play rugby. So I can take out the frustrations of the week, so I can have a run about. You know, this is what everybody plays it for. They like a run out. In a way, matching yourself physically against somebody else without getting beaten up in the process. I like a few pints afterwards you know – it helps keep you sane.

'You can go out there and you can forget. This is what I find. I can forget I'm having to save up; I can forget that I've got Val here; I can forget that I'm a teacher. I'm a rugby player, and that's all that matters. You can just cut yourself off for those eighty minutes, you can forget everything around you. It's escapism I suppose, in some way. But very necessary escapism – I get bored with myself. When I broke a finger I had six weeks off, I was fidgety, I didn't know what to do. It affected my job as well, 'cause I was on edge all the time. I wanted to get back. I wanted to play; I wanted to be out.

'The rest of my social life is spent here, at home, either sat watching the telly, or nattering, or going round to somebody's house for a chat, or something like that. Very suburban you know. Typical married man I suppose – when you take the rugby away. You set off for work at twenty past eight on a morning, you come back at six o'clock at night. You have tea. You sit down till eight o'clock with the kid – we watch telly together, she sits on my knee. Then, telly goes off, you do some work. Apart from the nights when I go training and I'm out, any other nights it's always spent here. I never go out apart from with Val, apart from when I go to the rugby club. On Sundays I work, preparing lessons – and you know, when you spend so much of your time preparing and stuff like that, if you can't work together or if you're not prepared to give and take over the working situation, well, your life would be hell.'

The 'game of marriage' – revolves around the 'give-and-take' of domestic dialogue: the 'little bit of rivalry which keeps us going'. In effect, the emotional security of the monogamous couple is carefully cultivated – part of a conscious familial 'project', based on assumption of mutual dependency:

'Most of the housework is done on a Friday night. I do the ironing and the cleaning, while Val does the baking. I help around the house a lot because if I didn't, she wouldn't be able to go out to work. I mean, it wouldn't be fair to expect her to do all the housework when she's out working. But this system, that we just sort of devised more than anything else, is just so that neither of us gets too tired. We just sort of pull our weight. But if she was at home all day, I don't think I'd lift a finger. I would expect it to be done. I would expect the meals to be cooked. But because she's out at work I'm prepared to pull my weight doing the housework. I'll do the washing up I suppose, decorating – I see decorating as part of my role in the game of marriage – I'll look after the car. You know, these sorts of things.

'It's security, knowing that someone needs you and you

need somebody else. You know, I need to be able to depend on somebody. I also like to think that person's dependent on me. I give, and I take, and I like to think that I give as much as I take. But at the moment I'm taking more than I'm giving – a lot more. I accept the fact; it bothers me, and it doesn't. I mean, when I'm at home it does, but when I'm taken out of the home situation and at school it doesn't. So I'm sort of torn.

'This house doesn't mean anything to me, 'cause it's not mine, I'm paying the council for it. But what's in it means a lot. The first couple of months it was, "now that's mine and that's her's" – but now it's our's. It took me quite a long time to relinquish what was mine to be our's. We laugh and joke about what's mine and what's our's and things like this. It's just playful antagonism, I suppose, on my part – saying that the car's mine. I know that it gets her narked – but not too narked, you know what I mean? We have a little bit of rivalry which sort of keeps us going. Well, everybody that gets married I suppose must go through that. You adjust to the situation. I think we both have. We've found out that our lives haven't changed that much, apart from the fact that we don't go out as much.

'But I mean, that's a choice we made – 'cause we want our own house. We could afford to go out – with our combined salaries we could afford to live it up. We could afford to have a new car, and all these sorts of things. But we want our own home. The thing is, the money I save, I may as well put it into something that's going to appreciate – and your house is going to appreciate over the long run. Plus the fact that I don't rate this as a "home" in the accepted sense of the word. You know, your own private plot. I mean there's some bloke living above me that comes down outside there, and every time he walks up and down I can hear him. It's not private in that respect.'

Alan recognizes that his life-style is fairly conventional. But he makes an important distinction between his 'social values' (explicit ideology) and 'mental attitudes'/'home attitudes' (the way his life is organized). It is primarily the latter, constituting the basic structure of his life, and including attitudes to career and family, that he is inclined to 'take-for-granted'. Here, he speaks of a 'block'. It is as though the structure, on certain levels, is independent of his will – all he can do is to try to keep a kind of 'equilibrium'. It is precisely at these levels that definitions of gender add their legitimacy to the status quo.

'I see my role as fifty per cent of a partnership, in providing for the home. Now I don't mean that I've got to earn exactly what she does, or that she's got to earn exactly what I do. But what goes into the house, the effort, has got to be fifty/fifty. But within that situation, you've got to be able to live your own life. I mean, I've got my life at the rugby club, where I can devoid myself of the family worries and the job. And you know, Val does her sewing and that sort of thing. I see a responsibility in keeping a job, whereas before I was married I could have just upped and left any job I'd got, for promotion, without thinking.

'You've got to maintain your own identity, or else you don't have a partnership. If one person rules the other then it's no longer a partnership, it becomes a monopoly. And once you've got one person dominating the other, especially with our characters – we're both very strong willed – it would lead to tension. And therefore she gives, and I give. You've got to do; you've got to back pedal. Otherwise it would be war.

'A lot of my values I've inherited from my parents. Not social values, I've got my own social code. Mental attitudes, home attitudes I think – you know, how a home should be run. I've inherited a lot of that from them because it's the only home I've known, and I keep what was good out of that and put it into this one. It's really difficult you see, because they're the sort of things that you take for granted – and when you start having to try and think of things which you take for granted, I don't know, I come up against a block. You see, I don't really associate my life in any way to my parents. But it's the way that it was always good if you owned your own house. I want to own my own house. Now I don't know how much of that is me wanting to own my own house – or what's been instilled into me that, you know, "You must own your own house". That's the type of thing where I don't know whether I'm influenced by my parents or not, or whether it's me. Things like keeping your bank balance in the black; making sure I'm well clothed and well fed; and then what's left over is spending money. I know I've inherited that. And I think the value of having a job. I was always told, "You must have a job; You must always earn your own money."

'I know when I get my own house that I shall be very much more stabilized – because that's the next goal in the out-of-career ladder, if you understand what I mean. I mean my career's going in that direction, and my home life's going in that direction, and I know what the next step up is in each direction, even though the career's got a fork in it. I'm open on two points there.

'They're both equal : but the career's more equal than home life. With a settled career, the home life goes hand in hand with it. But if I'm unsettled in my career, then I could see myself getting niggardly at home. So in that respect my career's more important than home life. But yet I couldn't work happily if I wasn't happy at home – so they're very much intertwined.

'And it's forms of relaxation that you need. To me it's relaxation playing rugby because I can get away. It's mental relaxation; it's certainly not physical relaxation – I come home knackered. But mentally I'm all right, you know, I've had that break. Somebody's sort of undone the stop-cap, and you know that the excess has drifted away. Screw it up again, and I'm all right again.'

Masculinity in the 'Progressive' Middle Class

In post-war Britain, the professional 'crisis of confidence' has affected all sections of the middle class. It is part of an ideological transformation – of cultural values and life-styles – that has followed from the decline of British imperialism. With less opportunity for colonial expansion, and with the collapse of the 'pioneering spirit', middle-class visions have narrowed to domestic, and personal, aspirations. As I have tried to show, this narrowing of vision is particularly felt at work – in the new cynicism of the bureaucrat; and the passing of ideals of 'duty', 'service', and 'honour'.

But the 'middle class' remains an alliance of heterogeneous social groups (owners of property, civil servants, managers, clerical workers) united more by ties of interest, than by immediately identical beliefs. For one sector in particular, which I shall term the 'progressive' middle class, the ideological uncertainty of the post-war period has carried far-reaching, even radical possibilities. For this class-fraction (which includes some teachers, social workers, journalists, creative artists) has developed a critical detachment from 'bourgeois' middle-class values. Against the virtues of thrift, self-denial, 'respectability', is projected a 'permissive' and spectacular 'counter-culture' – ranging from exotic habits of consumption (the 'colour-supplement' life-style), to alternatives to 'domesticity' (communal living, collective childcare). Replacing the conservative retreat to the home is a new, libertarian 'social conscience' – a 'new politics' of community action and civil rights.

This 'progressive' middle class is the product of an 'affluent' society. More than any other social group it has benefited from economic expansion: first, in the shift of capitalist production towards the stimulation of domestic demand; and second, in the growth of the 'non-productive' sector – the State Apparatus, particularly higher education. Of course, these are recent developments, and it is not possible to be altogether precise in their analysis. I am uncertain how far the 'progressive' middle class has become a sizeable proportion of the middle class as a whole, or how far it remains an influential 'fringe'. Another factor to be taken into account is regional variation: the 'progressive' middle class lives in big cities – especially London – and is more sporadic, even 'underground', in the still-respectable provinces.

Nevertheless, it is my impression that the 'progressive' middle class forms the 'vanguard' of contemporary capitalism. In the shifting focus of its experience, this class-fraction has explored the potentialities of consumerism – not just in terms of material demand (an appetite shared by the 'affluent' working class); but more especially in its total engagement with a 'culture' of gratification. Most of all, it is a projected vision of the 'good life' that has crystallized 'progressive' aspirations. It is an awareness of 'style' – the radical juxtaposition of cultural forms (East/West, Black/White) – that characterizes 'progressive' art, fashion, and music. Not all these activities are explicitly 'political', but in their spectacular construction they often do express a kind of self-consciousness. It is through this implicit self-consciousness that some (mainly youthful) middle-class consumers have begun to question the 'affluent society' itself.

For as it has confusingly unfolded, a vital element of post-war, middle-class culture has been a crisis of 'identification'. Growing up in the 'fifties and 'sixties was like passing through a gallery of mirrors – at every point you confronted an image of yourself, instantaneously, but in a distorted form. The image brought your fantasy to life, but was itself fragmented, and manipulated – part of a contrived sensation. In the very moment of consumption, between the image and the sensation, there was a fleeting awareness of emptiness – a gap between the promise and the reward. Even at the height of the experience, in the full glitter of its neon lighting, there persisted the sense of being 'taken for a ride'.

As the consumer boom has faded, it has become possible to perceive its contradictions. The pre-packaged myth of 'happiness' ('You've never had it so good') masked a lingering anxiety. This anxiety was understood by feminists: a celluloid sexuality glamorized the 'dolly bird', but existed uneasily beside the traditional 'myth of motherhood'. For men on the other hand (since masculine feelings are typically displaced, into a self-indulgent or theatrical 'anguish' which conceals their social meaning) disenchantment remained undefined. But partly the realities of work have continued to reproduce masculine insecurities; and partly male fantasies of 'sexual freedom' have disintegrated. Finally, in the 'seventies, it has become possible to comprehend that spirit of cynicism and self-pity which for so long has characterized the masculine 'counter-culture':

'They are spoonfeeding Casanova, to get him to feel more assured, then they'll kill him with self-confidence, after poisoning him with words.'

(Bob Dylan: *Desolation Row*)

The first indications of a masculine emotional crisis became apparent through the experience of war. The suffering of the First World War – as new destructive machinery confronted the anachronistic strategy of trench warfare – is now part of our cultural heritage. But there was also an experience of the Second World War, less apparent in sheer human sacrifice, more a matter of temperament, which has had a 'hidden' historical significance. During the war a feeling of disbelief began to undermine the unquestioning will to fight. This war was the last moment of 'high' British imperialism: it fostered the growth of cynicism, of satire, even a cult of the 'anti-hero' – which was to surface in the 'fifties with the Goons and the Angry Young Men. Perhaps the modern army was too mechanized, too impersonal, to foster an awareness of physical combat. Possibly the involvement of women in the province of men penetrated the soldier's vain-glory. But certainly, for many sections of the middle class, the Second World War shattered the prestige of an imperialist masculinity. As the novels of Doris Lessing show so well, a man's presence, towards women, began to seem petty and absurd:

'Douglas, in khaki with the pack on his shoulder, a red-brown man with fat knees a good stone heavier than he had been, and reeking of beer, had seemed to her gross and commonplace. His round, rather fat face, grinning proudly at her, had been a revelation of what he really was ... It was quite impossible that this man should be her husband. She was married to one of the boys; he would always, all his life, be one of the boys. At sixty he would still be a schoolboy ... The condition of being a woman in wartime, she thought angrily, was that one should love not a man, but a man in relation to other men. Whether it was Douglas with the boys, or the boys of the Air Force, it was all the same – and it was precisely this thing, dangerous and attractive, which fed the intoxication of war, heightened the pulse, and drugged them all into losing their heads. You loved not a man, but that man's idea of you in relation to his friends.'

(Doris Lessing, 1965:577–8)

This experience of the Second World War was perpetuated by

a generation of post-war fathers, who, in 1945, came home to get married. They brought back, to provincial Britain, memories of Asia, of Africa, and the 'intoxicating' experience of being with 'the boys'. From their wives they demanded a belief in the validity of their six-year adventure. But their one-sided dream of 'home' masked the potential clash of perspectives, the disbelief, which Doris Lessing describes. Beneath its idyllic facade, family life required a complex readjustment – a language of emotional sensitivity which 'the boys' did not possess :

'He suddenly picked her brushes and hand mirror off the table and flung them crashing against the wardrobe. She remained still ... She looked steadily at him, and knew she was no longer afraid of him. She had been – very afraid. It was because – she saw this from the inward-looking gleam in the puffed eyes – he had slid over into that mood of self-controlled hysteria which she knew so well. It was as if he were saying to invisible onlookers, "Look how I'm treated! Look how I'm behaving!" It was with her nerves that she understood that it was not genuine. She waited for him to speak.'

(Doris Lessing, 1965:655–6)

It is important to remember that the teenagers of the 'permissive 'sixties' were the children of men like Douglas. Whether violent or philosophical, these men no longer believed in themselves or the world for which they had fought. To the feast of consumerism they introduced a nervousness which checked its indulgent gaiety. And for many children of the war, or its immediate aftermath, this was their paternal legacy; as the seeds of disillusionment sown by fathers began to bear fruit in their children's 'counter-culture'.

For many sons, the legacy of the war pervaded the patriarchal vision. The model of masculinity seemed to resist any simple 'identification'. Where the professional 'crisis of confidence' had already begun to undermine its ethical justification, an unquestioning sense of 'duty' was no longer possible; and this feeling was intensified by awareness of the insecurity of one's father. Partly the awareness was real, for the war actually did interrupt many middle-class careers; but partly it was imaginary, a response to the anti-heroism of the reconstructed society. The

114

son's dependency on, and involvement within, the unstable career of his father, was coupled with his critical detachment, and search for an 'alternative' life-style.

The outcome of this search was a conception of 'anti-work', which for some men, positively broke away from old 'careerist' preoccupations. Sustained by a sense of 'authenticity' – 'doing your own thing' – it seemed possible to give up the rat-race and to cultivate a trade, a small farm, or to become a community worker. This 'drop-out' syndrome of the 'sixties, was far more than an idle response to 'affluence'; it was a critical rejection of the traditional middle-class ethic. Dropping-out was personally difficult for men committed to compulsive work and dreams of future security. However transitory, it made conscious the latent pressure of the middle-class masculine role. But it also gave a man the space to think or travel, to reformulate his priorities. For middle-class men especially, it prefigured the possibility of part-time work, with a less obsessive attitude to the home.

This piecemeal relaxation of middle-class masculinity was paralleled by the struggle for women's emancipation. From the first stirrings of an alternative consciousness in the Second World War, middle-class women, have developed the potentialities of the 'affluent society'. Pursuing careers outside the home, women have not only been forced to challenge male chauvinism at work; but also the 'myth of motherhood' which represents the patriarchal definition of their role. Against the stereotyped imagery of advertising and fashion, feminists have asserted their sexual autonomy. In some sectors of the middle class, women have begun, concretely, the long fight to destroy patriarchal culture – partly by maintaining a psychological independence of men; and partly by breaking with the family. Even the 'cosmopolitan' housewife, rearing her children with Dr Spock, consuming her whole-foods, and practising her yoga, has a 'progressive' vision of herself – to set against the stoicism of her mother's generation.

In its outcome therefore, for this class-fraction as a whole, the post-war world has pinpointed a socio-sexual *contradiction*. The crisis of middle-class masculinity is counterposed to the emancipation of middle-class women. As insecure careerists, as dropouts, for the historical and social reasons I have outlined, middle-class men have been growing more and more dependent on images of domesticity; just as women themselves have been breaking these images apart. And this socio-sexual contradiction has inevitably been experienced, especially by women, as a bitter struggle. Women have only been able to assert their independence at the expense of men, who were, so to speak, moving in the opposite direction. For this reason, although the contradiction between men and women has been felt in all aspects of middle-class life – from the office to the classroom – its principle site has been the *family*, where the two trajectories have directly collided.

Today, the middle-class family is the focal point of a political struggle. For the contradiction between the sexes has exposed its three main points of stress – the relationship of the married couple, relations between parents and children, and the experience of sexuality itself. Women have been in the vanguard of this change because for them undermining the myth of domesticity is a prerequisite for equality with men. But although many men have resisted – with clichéd accusations of 'penis-envy'; with humourless chauvinist jokes about 'womens libbers'; and, when the chips are down, with overt emotional blackmail and aggression – some men have begun to recognize the importance of personal changes. The difficulty with this realization has been that, even where the middle-class couple has self-consciously tried to 'equalize', and even where liberal men have voluntarily surrendered their privileges, there have persisted unconscious limitations, built into masculinity itself.

In some sectors of the 'progressive' middle class, there has arisen a new ideology of the couple, organized around notions of 'companionship' or 'partnership', or what some sociologists call 'joint conjugal roles'. They argue that with the benefits of a consumer society, the modern wife can become a 'truly equal marriage partner' with a serious career of her own. This leads to a process of 'role equalization'; demanding first, that the husband looks after children and does housework, and second, that he accepts, in a general way, his wife's 'autonomy' to develop her own interests. This is the classic 'dual-career family',

116

a full-time project for both partners – and according to the liberal view, achievable with planning and tolerance. In January 1973, for example, an article appeared in the *Sunday Times* asking:

'Anyone for Open Marriage?:
With all the stress that modern life imposes on marriage it ought to be coming apart at the seams. It isn't; yet the institution is changing in ways still hardly understood or defined, and it will surely change further as the new forces on it dig deeper.

'The situation is confusing but it is exciting; new possibilities are presenting themselves for a meaningful and satisfying relationship ...

'The ideal would be a genuine sharing of responsibilities both in the outside world and at home, as home-makers and parents. Husbands and wives would share the domestic burdens and the financial burdens ... It presupposes a *real* equality for women – and men accepting that equality. It would also undoubtedly be made more feasible with the arrival of a genuinely shorter working week, with husbands and wives working at part-time jobs, and filling in for each other at home.'

(Susan Raven, 1973)

It is perhaps the 'ideal' middle-class 'solution' – but 'progressive' couples have increasingly found that they cannot simply 'equalize' by exchanging traditional roles. Much more is at stake, for men, as the inherited power to patronize is irrevocably surrendered. Liberal men, who are otherwise open to change, and who would willingly surrender their career motivation, still feel guilty as they catch themselves out assuming the right to make decisions, or rationalizing their partner's problems. Here, an 'open marriage' comes face to face with traditional 'domesticity' – defining social interactions in conscious attitudes, and also unconsciously, in terms of personal identity. The apparent 'equality' of marriage – mystified by religious and romantic vows of 'love' – masks its discriminatory character. Keith Paton has written of the '60/40 game' – the persistence, even within

117

an 'open marriage' of masculine strategies for 'avoiding the issue':

'To play this game you admit that she is the aggrieved partner, you are the guilty partner. Relatively – because we've all got our hang-ups haven't we now? Yes, well OK, the way I look at it is this: whenever we disagree or row, you are right most of the time – 60 to 70% say. But of course, if you grant there are some things I can see and you can't, in any particular case I might be right. You've admitted the possibility. Well I just think I'm right about this one. And (funnily enough) all other cases the same. So in the end I don't give an inch.

'Men insist on fragmenting their power, their bloodymindedness, into a hundred little issues – on each of which (once safely parcelled out) they are prepared to argue rationally. It's just that she gets so worked up. She is getting emotional because she knows "the issue" is not *the issue*.'

(Keith Paton, 1973)[1]

To be inside a married couple, however 'open' the marriage, is to be part of a mutual negotiation. And one of the more insidious tendencies of the middle-class male is a liberalism which conceals, but in the end reproduces, his traditional power. What might have been a genuine effort at 'companionship' is compromised by a new 'moralism' – the *gift* of freedom to women: 'Of course dear, it's right for you to have your interests, as long as you recognize my right to mine.' Such 'benevolence' fails to take into account the underlying power-structure within which the 'gift' is made. It is a claustrophobic, privatized dialogue, where 'negotiation' assumes a perpetual momentum, and which is maintained by the couple as an institution. Men hang on to this institution, not simply for chauvinist motives, or because they do not possess the personal courage to change, but because they cannot foresee a future beyond its determination.

Can the children of 'open marriages' look forward to a less determined future? Certainly since the war, the middle class

[1] In *Brothers*, a Men's Liberation Newsletter – see 'Suggestions for further reading'.

has experimented with a 'progressive' approach to childcare, which is openly dynamic in its use of space, in its attitude to 'free-expression', and in its concealment of more overt forms of discipline. In a 'progressive' classroom, the authority structure is implicit, masked by a variety of materials (different kinds of creative games, drama, artistic experimentation). The school itself is part of a social-democratic 'community' which, according to its apologists, begins to encourage a 'symmetrical' family structure. Pinpointing the plight of children who are the product of their parents' 'brief encounter with their biological urges', Young and Willmott foresee a move to collective forms of childcare – in preschool nurseries, creches, and, in some cases, communes:

> 'Children coming from homes fragmented by the new triumphs of technology and feminism might fail to develop into the kind of people capable of making a centre of peace in the homes that they in their turn would establish for their children to be reared in ... Alternative forms of housing and alternative styles of communal living are needed as much as more nursery schools. Not everyone wants, or will want, to be stuck into the conventional home. But we do not expect that communes and the like will provide for more than small numbers. In view of what has happened in other countries it seems unlikely that any large-scale substitute of this kind will be found for the family.'
>
> (Michael Young and Peter Willmott, 1973 : 280–82)

At best then, the 'alternative' remains ambiguous. 'Progressive' social-democracy is committed to reform, but is uncertain of its challenge to the domestic 'centre of peace'. There persists a residual individualism – a distrust of collective identity. And the removal, in 'symmetrical families' of an explicit parental authority (its association with punishment, and fear) still fails to touch the parental 'investment' in the child. Men particularly want sons. They glorify the role of progenitor – the 'bond' between father and son. There remain mysterious feelings of protection, responsibility, and recognition (support in distress, praise in achievement) which over-determine the biological relationship.

As a non-parent, I find this relationship difficult to comprehend. Few liberal parents will today talk of 'maternal instincts' or 'natural bonds'. But there remains the collusive structure which displaces the non-parent (to the role of 'babysitter' or 'family friend'). And a critical attitude to childcare still often seems to stop short at the point where 'security' is threatened. Children themselves have a knack of testing the contradictions in parental experiments – even in 'progressive' families, where they are encouraged to 'explore' for themselves, there persists a prohibitive 'guiding hand'. But perhaps the most paradoxical of all 'progressive' attitudes is a recognition that, finally, authoritarian and sexual stereotypes seem inescapable : children themselves seem to demand them as a means to identification. As one 'progressive' father has written :

'I remember a game. I am a giant, hulking, apelike. The children squeal and run, abandoning themselves for a moment to the sensation of flight and terror. I drop to all fours, descend into the animal. Some of them clamber on to my back, start to beat me about the head and shoulders. The others join in, squirming into the heap. Their faces express stern determination, cunning, savage joy ...

'The game is about fear and mastery. There is nothing collective about the children's response. When they run away they push and jostle, and when they fight they do it with complete absorption. It is a private fear and an individual mastery.

'For me, and for them too perhaps, the game is also about fathers and maleness. Coming down to hands and knees ... I pass in a regressive movement from parent to child. And the children, overcoming me, in the same moment realize the violence implicit in the size and strength of the parent ... (They seem) to approach and challenge one of the borderlines of identity : the difference between parent and child.'

(Birmingham Women's Liberation Playgroup, 1975) [2]

Contradictions within sexual behaviour have also been a central problem for the 'progressive' middle-class. In the post-

[2] In *Out of the Pumpkin Shell*, Running a Women's Liberation Playgroup – see 'Suggestions for further reading'.

war consumer boom, sex was sold as fashion, as cosmetics, as pop, and as pornography. The promise of sex was interwoven with a consumer world of cars and penthouse flats. For some men this was the ultimate heroic age – as the quest for sexual 'experience' demanded a mastery of sexual 'technique'. To be able to 'handle' one's women, to be 'good in bed', was an essential part of colour-supplement manhood.

And yet the Laurentian formula for sexual emancipation – without reserves or defences – was never, in practice, achieved. Because of the ways 'permissive sexuality' was defined – partly in a preoccupation with orgasm; partly in the voyeurism of nudity; partly in the emphasis on technique – the real problem of the significance of sexuality in social relationships was largely ignored. Progressive middle-class liberalism demanded sexual freedom for women as well as men; but sexual passion was still acted out in familiar terms of masculine 'conquest' – to which women could only 'respond'. Although many men took their ideals seriously, seeking 'free women' who lived for themselves and their careers – in bed they still demanded submission and the affirmation of masculinity. Clancy Sigal, in an interview with the leader of the 144 Piccadilly squat (1969), elicited the classically contradictory responses of the progressive middle-class male:

'CS: "Does a young man ever go without?"

FH: "Very rare, unless he is on the road."

CS: "Is it nice for the girls?"

FH: "It depends on how good a lover the man is. Emotionally it cannot be very satisfying for the women because they don't receive any sense of security, fulfilment or satisfaction. And a women needs this."

CS: "Have you found preferences for a certain kind of woman? Have you gone back to the kind of woman your parents would have approved?"

FH: "Not really. The woman I want is one who can sing nicely. The old-fashioned sort of woman ... It's very difficult to define ... a girl ... a social worker, or something like this. She must be reasonably intelligent, capable of communication, conversation and stimulation, and this form of person will be sympathetic to the ideals I hold anyway." ²

(Clancy Sigal, 1969)

Again, it was a case of women being offered their freedom by men, on men's terms – presupposing feminine dependency. The sexual 'liberation' offered with one hand was, in the same movement, removed by the other.

This 'permissive' sexual mirage was more than a male-chauvinist conspiracy. The definitions of advertisers, pop-stars, even squatters, were rooted in an established middle-class culture. Both sexes had inherited the bourgeois dream of romantic love, whose character was inherently one-sided. The passivity or narcissism of traditional femininity 'mirrored' the self-glorious potency of men. Masculine dominance required feminine subordination, freedom produced jealousy, independence sought dependence, in ever more complex 'knots' of mutual mystification : 'I am dependent on you, but I don't let it show, because you want me to be independent of you, even though you, wishing you were independent, are dependent on me,' etc. These were socially-reproduced feelings, contained within the shell of the nuclear family. This was the immediate form in which sexual feeling appeared, and at first, the only context in which it could be understood.

But the compromise between masculine domination and sexual 'permissiveness' could not last for ever. The inherent precariousness of liberal masculinity was put to the test by women themselves, who, in the Women's Liberation Movement have collectively constructed a new sexual identity. Not only were the prevailing images of sexuality 'equalized'; they were also subverted and transformed – redefined by a politicized feminist consciousness. There was a new search for integrated patterns of sexuality, outside the restrictions of monogamy, beyond the psychological splits required to act out the contradictory expectations of men. As women found a new self-confidence, their search began to involve men, who could not ignore this challenge to their expectations :

'Of course I'm jealous. Naive sucker that I am, I never expected this pain. I never expected this unceasing ache and emptiness, these explosions into almost delirious anguish. I never expected I would feel so crushed, so left out, so insecure, so inadequate, so lonely, so *paranoid*.

'But why? Is it really such a naive question? What is this emotion that means the more somebody I love is happy, the more miserable I feel? She is more confident more fulfilled, more *herself* than I ever remember – and hate it. Why?'

(John Miles, 1973)

For 'progressive' middle-class men, masculinity itself is in a crisis. Feeling of sexual jealousy are inescapable; they feed upon themselves and destroy a man's emotional life. In the post-war world, the economic exploitation of sexuality – a profusion of images, invitations, hints of seduction, and gratification – has by itself undermined monogamous 'possession'. The tantalizing face of publicity, the focus of contemporary arts, and, most significantly, the main preoccupation of an urban, flat-dwelling life-style – sexual fulfilment has become a middle-class dream. As this dream has been taken by women beyond the compromise of a male-oriented 'permissiveness', at its core is revealed again the masculine fear of failure. As he loses self-control, the 'paranoia' of the jealous lover is intensified; he is threatened not by an external force, but by the personal surrender of his exclusive sexual power.

Tom is an Irish emigré, living in Manchester. For several years he worked as a civil engineer. He was, as he says, successful; moving into the 'hierarchy of engineers' – making deals, entertaining. There were managerial pressures, ambiguous relationships, moral dilemmas – but these were over-shadowed by the commitment to working, sustained by family responsibilities.

It was when Tom's wife, Sue, joined the Women's Movement, and Tom himself began to make friends outside the engineering world, that he became aware of the burden of his career. In the context of a 'progressive' middle-class 'counter-culture' (encounter groups, play-groups, women's liberation); and through an acceptance, within the family, of experiment and change; Tom was able to discover a new world of domestic and personal 'alternatives'.

123

Looking back on his working life, Tom describes his managerial responsibilities. On the one hand, as site engineer, he was confronted with a stream of practical problems. On the other, as site agent, he was obliged to negotiate with council officials and higher management. Like many junior managers, Tom maintained an ambiguous 'face'; partly as 'one of the men on the job', and, partly where necessary, the firm's diplomatic representative. The role has an in-built assumption of gamesmanship – 'there's a sort of battle going on all the time' – with rules which are taken for granted. It requires an accidental breaking of the rules, the shock of a death, to recognize the full extent of the human sacrifice they demand:

'I was a civil engineer. Site agent in fact, which meant complete control of a building site. I was the site engineer and agent combined, which entailed the actual setting out of the work – I mean in terms of lines, levels and heights, and the ordering of materials; and just generally seeing that people knew what they had to do. Passing instructions on to a site foreman, who would then carry them out. On a really big project everything would be divided up in sections and you'd have section engineers, and section foremen, and then there'd be the site agent who'd be ultimately responsible for the whole of the site. But the firm I worked for did smaller type work.

'Part of the job, working on the site, was actually measurement, and getting paid for it. I mean, this is a very important part, measuring the work up and meeting council officials, and working out exactly what has been done. You do particular things and they're all measured as you do them. You go round with a council official and sort of agree that this has been done, and then it would be marked in and paid for.

'But it's a funny sort of relationship. I mean, he's in a very powerful position, so that on the one hand you're hating his guts, and on the other you're always having to be diplomatic. He is basically there to give you the least amount of money. I mean they see their job as very important in the sense that this is, you know, taxpayers' money, and they're not going to give it out. And my job really is to get as much as I can for the least amount of work, or for no work at all. There's this sort of battle going on all the time, a perpetual argument on how the work should be done. Like, if you're putting six inches of concrete, he will come down and say, "Well look I think there's eight inches of concrete. I want to see eight inches of concrete there." You say, "Of course, I'll see to it right away" – at the back of your head thinking as soon as he's gone again, you'll tell them to cut down on it. 'Cause this is how the small firms operate. I mean they undercut the big firm to get the job, and then they're faced with the problem of how to make a profit. And he knows it – all the time he knows that you're out to cut corners.

'And there are other things, like safety for example. It's his job to see that you carry out safety requirements. But you get no money for doing things in a safe fashion, and we couldn't afford to do it. I mean, there was no money to buy the types of shoring. What happens is you decide to dig a trench, and as you move along you put steel props into it, and there's a strut going from either side, and you just wind them up. And you keep doing that all the way along. It's a very slow process, and it's very difficult to work in conditions like that. Most of the men don't like it either. I mean, they don't like doing it for a start, and they don't like working in it because it's so incredibly difficult to get the pipes and anything else into it. So if for example you're doing a trenching in fairly solid ground, you think it's safe. You make this decision yourself.

'What happened in one particular case was that a load of concrete came round, was delivered, and the driver of the lorry drove right up to the side of the trench, which was a stupid thing to do. And the trench started to collapse. And there was about a dozen people down in it and they all sort of ran out. But one chap ran the opposite direction and got completely covered, both with the lorry and the three or four tons of earth on top of him. About half a dozen people started digging him up then but he was dead. I was there actually, and I put my hand down, and could feel this clump of hair, and sort of dug round his head, and there's just this blue face looking up. I suppose I felt responsible. Plus the fact that I had to go to the coroner's court and give evidence. And in the coroner's court they could have returned a verdict of manslaughter, in the sense that the accident wouldn't have happened had the trench been properly shored. Again I mean the driver was incredibly stupid in driving up, and he was as responsible as anyone else. Then the firm was responsible. But this happens every day. Maybe there are not accidents every day, but every firm commits something. The men accept it. That's the thing especially about Irish labourers in fact. They're fatalistic about it. I mean, it's nobody's fault – it just happens.'

Unlike manual labour, managerial work is a personal obligation. The 'responsible boss' assumes he is indispensable; and he lives for his work. As Tom describes, there is an ambiguous extension of 'work' into 'social life' – winning contracts, repeating gossip, reaffirming the masculine culture of the engineering world. For the aspiring careerist, it is as important that he be able to perpetuate the conversation, as it is that he display his competence 'on the job'.

'I liked contacts with the men. I mean I used to play cards with them. Because they were Irish too you see, lots of similarities in a way. I think I found it very difficult to assume the role of the boss. I used to work it another way, that the boss was somewhere out there, and that we were all, sort of, workers. I found that in terms of getting the job done it was as good as, and better in fact, that the hard line – which tends to be the case with most civil engineering bosses because there is such a change over of labour.

'So in terms of results I was quite good at being a civil engineer. I could make money and get the job done very fast. But I never felt that I was doing it for the firm, if you know what I mean. I think the bosses regarded me in a slightly suspicious fashion. I never got involved in the inner circles of the company. You know, I was never the sort of blue-eyed boy. This is what I felt myself. I didn't want to be one. I don't think I fitted into the role – the role of the civil engineer didn't come very easy to me at all. I used to have real battles with it, in terms of the civil engineering way of life, and the hard drinking, and the talk about "getting the men to do things" — and just the whole structure of it really. I suppose it's what I think of as management. I never saw myself fitting into management. I mean, just that the people who work there don't matter at all, the important thing is to make money.

'There was the sort of politics of engineering too you know. I mean it's a sort of world of its own. You know all the other contracts that are going on in the town. You know a lot of engineers too, working for different companies. And of course the client, which usually was the corporation, would know as well. And he'd be telling little stories of what happened here, and how much money such and such was making, or the really good stories were how much such a company was losing. That was the favourite. Who'd gone bankrupt, and who was on the verge of bankruptcy. And the engineers in your own company who he either liked or disliked.

'There had to be quite a lot of socializing done between the company and the client and this entailed taking people out to dinner regularly. You always took them out to dinner after you'd done a measurement, which was probably once a month. We all had an expense account, a fairly big expense account, because there's a hell of a lot of money involved in all this. Real big sums of money. And this was a very very important part of the work. They really saw it in those terms, not only if they weren't taken out to a meal, but it also had to be quite a spread. I remember you'd do a measurement which would start at nine o'clock in the morning and go on till about twelve, and then everything would stop and you'd go out to one of the plush hotels on the outskirts of Manchester, and there would be everything laid on. We'd all go out and have a real big spread. I think there again I never did quite fit in the conversation. And I mean I remember trying hard, I remember trying to be good at it, as it were.

'Wives were never brought in, they were excluded. Which I think is different from a lot of other companies, where the wife is very much involved. So people recounted their sexual exploits. I mean, manly talk, just jokes. And coming round Christmas or something like that, the company would lay on a party. This would be for some of the people in the other engineering companies, and mainly for the corporation themselves. All the beer would be free for a start, and there'd be lashings of food. And there'd be strip shows – but I mean, high quality strip. They'd take place in various clubs in and around Manchester, usually just on the outskirts. I remember one in a sort of back room of one of these hotels. This was a private showing, where in fact women were brought in to entertain. And not only did they do a sort of strip show, but some of the men got involved sexually with the women as well too. That was allowed. The men actually took their clothes off and got stuck in. This was the real high class. It was only done for very favourable council officials. I've actually got memories of these things and they're terrible really. You see because these people get their beer for nothing there'd be just these sort of three-quarter filled glasses lying around, crumbs sitting on top of them. They were so bloody greedy that they wouldn't actually finish a drink at all.'

As he moved up the 'ladder', Tom felt his life to be splitting apart. There were ambivalences in the job itself; moving from engineering as such to 'wheeling and dealing around money'. There were ethical dilemmas; feeling the commitment to work, but questioning its social values. It seemed that the practical aspects of work maintained an intolerably false and decadent 'superstructure'. At first, with a psychological commitment to the 'real man's world' it was impossible for Tom to articulate his uncertainty. Only, with Sue's support, by making a practical break, could he gain a critical perspective on his situation:

'Once I started moving up the hierarchy I started getting involved in the actual making of money, in the wheeling and dealing around money. But then I did feel a bit ambiguous about that as well, because I felt I actually enjoyed part of that, in a funny sort of way. I mean in a lot of other companies you would never see that side of it. You'd just do your job, and all that would go on you would certainly have no knowledge of it. I could never see myself just doing that. I suppose I'm a bit contradictory there in some ways, but I was into the idea of being successful and getting on. I mean this is the natural progression in the civil engineering world, where you do sort of move up that ladder.

'And then I think the break started to come. I became very friendly with a teacher, who of course had a very different life than I had, and spent a lot of time at home, and on lots of holidays. I remember we used to go to the pub regularly on Monday night, and with some other teachers as well too. And I used to go back to his house afterwards and talk till about three or four o'clock, just in a philosophical way I suppose – which I enjoyed a lot, sort of talking, just about things other than civil engineering. I started to realize then that I was missing out on lots of things. But I don't think I was ever attracted to what he was doing, because, I mean, there was something about civil engineers who felt that they were really where it was at. I mean, this hard life – a real man's world this was, where you worked hard and drank hard, and then there was lots of money floating around.

'So I started to live a completely split life – split in terms of I worked because I felt I had to work, just to earn money, but there was no feedback. I lived a completely different social life. And I think I met a few people who had actually given up work, and just hearing about them somehow made it real, I mean that it was a possibility. But again I think the important thing is that I never "gave up" work in that sense. I never sort of said, "Well this is it. Finished." I became aware of it only after I'd done it, and discovered that it was possible to live without working as an engineer. There was this feeling before that my whole world would collapse around me if I stopped working.

'In retrospect it was a sort of little experiment – that I was going to give up the particular job I was doing, just to see what it was like for a couple of weeks, three weeks, a month. And I remember saying this to Sue in fact, but she didn't like the idea at all. 'Cause at this time she was very anti the work I was doing. I suppose she suffered from it – every day I'd come home and say how awful it had been. She wanted me to give up the whole civil engineering, whereas I think in fact I was saying, "Well, I'll give it up now but I'll go back to it again."[2]

Tom's emerging perspective was supported by a network of 'alternative' social activities. In and around Manchester, in the late 'sixties, there had developed an informal 'counter-culture' – of radical groups, publications, ideas. Developing his earlier contact with the group of teachers, Tom became a 'claimant', joined an encounter group, and took his children to the local play-centre. As he explains, he was substantially influenced by Sue's commitment to Women's Liberation:

'In between that time I had started to do other things – what those other things are I'm not quite sure at the moment – but I suppose making other relationships outside work, meeting other people. So on the one hand there was this real empty space when I gave up work – I mean I just didn't know what to do with myself really, sort of kicking my heels. And yet I had been doing a few things before this, and so I was meeting other people. I'd gone to this encounter group while I was at work. And I was involved in encounter groups as an ongoing thing.

'And then there was this involvement about trying to stay out of work. I mean, I think I got involved in Social Security. I made that my little work. Part of the week was on Wednesday's when I signed on, and I took David and it was a sort of outing. You set off and sign on, and that took up half a day. And I suppose I was taken up with just thinking what I can do; my thoughts were, "Now that I've given up, what am I going to do?"[2] I suppose I started to read quite a bit more, wanting to talk about books I'd read. I started voluntary probation work. And I got involved in the playgroup as well. Two days a week I used to do it. That was an incredibly packed week somehow, or so it seemed at the time.

'I suppose it did come through Sue. Sue was very much into Women's Liberation. I suppose it took up the best part of her life really. You know, her whole social life was around Women's Liberation. I think there was a sort of breakdown in the division of labour in the household – in the sense that

I was forced into sharing the housework. I say forced in the sense that I mean it was a case of seeing that I was there, that I spent as much time in the house as Sue did, and there seemed to be no reason why I shouldn't do it. I think I looked round for reasons why I shouldn't do it, but I couldn't come up with any. And it became very important that I formed some politics around that, I mean to myself. Child-care was sort of being collectivized at that time, you know, playgroups. They had a playgroup going in Manchester and it went on in different people's houses on different days. As I said before, I started going to the playgroup and I went along because I enjoyed it and it was something to do, and yet on the other hand I felt that this isn't really work. I mean this isn't man's work. There was this sort of split going on. But then, feeling it was important that I was doing the things I was doing, in terms of Women's Liberation, in terms of the ideas that they had about kids.'

What Tom describes here – moving from an unquestioned routine to an 'alternative' life-style, is a period of transition. The period itself has two principle characteristics: a growing 'consciousness', of the restrictions imposed by work, and the relation between work and home; and a sense of 'choice', or 'freedom' – a feeling that it's possible to change his own destiny. Of course, in a world without fixed boundaries, the awareness of freedom can itself be highly problematic, uncovering as many difficulties as it resolves. In his own account Tom hints at a personal confrontation with his future, 'responsible' only to himself, without the stability he assumed in his former situation. But, by the same token, it is only by sacrificing the fixed goals of his career that he is able to conceive a future for himself. Through his own self-consciousness he experiences a new quality in his personal relationships:

'I think my relationship with Sue has changed from what it was before. I mean, I feel now that we have a relationship. I feel now that it's changed so much, but that we've developed a relationship in the last couple of years, as opposed to just being side by side.

'I think it's interesting too how I've got a much stronger relationship with David, because I was around when he was very young – as opposed to Katie, who I probably only saw for an hour each day, when she went to bed. I suppose I think Katie relates much more strongly to Sue that she does to me. But then it's really difficult to know. I suppose when I was working I didn't have the time to be around so much. And I think I was very much into traditional father and mother type relationships, where I would certainly read bedtime stories, but that's really as far as it went. I did what most fathers do. I remember I never felt very comfortable in that role either – the father, and what fathers should do ... discipline.

'And I mean, I don't think I ever did try to understand Sue. I assumed a lot. I felt that she was basically quite unhappy in her role as a wife and mother. She was only eighteen when we got married, so in a sense she had missed out on a very important part of her life. She was thrown straight into this role, and it was a very frustrating time. And in some ways I was responsible for that. And there didn't seem any way out of it. So in some ways it was better not to try and understand it. And I think she probably felt the same about me; that after a while she wasn't interested in the work I was doing anyway, and she picked up that I was getting unhappy in the work, and there didn't seem to be any point in trying to understand it because there didn't seem any alternatives.

'And now there's lots of alternatives. I don't know if they will ever materialize. But there's this feeling that, you know, we have sort of control over our lives, in the sense that we didn't have before. I mean, I think it's amazing, the few choices people have, or the few choices they feel, or that they haven't any choice at all. And this is coming back to leaving work too. I think it was at that point when I thought, "Christ, I'm going to be doing this for the rest of my life; I just can't do it anymore."

'I think that this was probably tied in with always feeling that I had to earn the money. And I think as I stopped doing that, and the money was coming from somewhere else, and I wasn't necessarily the one who was getting it either – I stopped feeling this need to be the provider. I'm not sure how much is tied in with my idea that I should be working – that it wasn't right not to be working – and how strong this was, as opposed to just earning the money to keep a wife and family. I never felt I had a strong male identity. I could never possibly be in a relationship where I was seen to be the one who had to earn the money. I could never see it happening in my relationship now. I think that is positive in the sense that I feel the other feeling is a negative feeling. I think there's a certain freedom in that.

'I suppose you're responsible only to yourself. I can see the future now, whereas before I don't think I ever actually thought that much about the future. I think I see myself as very mobile now. I think both of us feel this way. We're not tied, we don't have the same restrictions, and jobs. And I mean if we don't seem to be getting anything from being together, there seems little point in staying together, because we don't have the same sorts of restrictions as we had before. I think that's what's quite nice about it now, in the sense that we certainly don't see ourselves spending the next twenty years together. I should think it would be very unlikely in fact. So all in all, you know, the world's my oyster.'

Tom's narrative points the way to my final chapter. For his account, of the experience of self-discovery, questions the implicit structure of the masculine world. Because 'work' and 'home' are interdependent, changes in one sphere dictate changes in the other – a total transformation of everyday life. And Tom's discovery of widening horizons is perhaps a proto-type for other disillusioned middle-class men.

Equally however, there are some difficult questions, which insinuate themselves 'through' Tom's narrative – beneath the surface of its apparent optimism. What is the wider significance of such a privileged experience? Is this simply one, 'progressive' middle-class adjustment to circumstances? If masculinity is structured, as we have seen, in socio-historical terms, what is the status of the individual solution? What, in short, is the *political* validity of Tom's personal account?

4

The limits of masculinity

'Nowadays a woman's gotta hit a man – to make him know she's there.'

(Captain Beefheart: *Clear Spot*)

I have mentioned, in my introductory chapter, the feminist practice of 'consciousness-raising', and have suggested its significance for men. In this final chapter I want to examine this suggestion, in the light of my experience as a member of a men's group. I want to argue that the experience of masculinity, in its social dimensions and historical shifts, can be clarified within a consciousness-raising group. The small group, ideally, provides a bridge between (often inarticulate, undefined) personal experience, and a collective, social context in which it is shared and can be analysed.

I am not claiming that there are any necessary parallels between men's groups, and the politics of Women's Liberation. In this sense, since it is a feminist political practice, to talk about 'men's consciousness-raising' is perhaps misleading. I retain the definition in this account, partly because it was adopted by our group in Birmingham; and partly because it does, still, capture the process of 'becoming conscious' (a growing 'self-consciousness') of murky, unconscious areas in personal experience. This, however, is not a feminist consciousness – constructed from a position of social subordination. Men remain the 'subjects', in dominance, of a patriarchal culture. Whereas for women 'becoming conscious' is therefore a *political* struggle (with negative self-images, and *against* the power of men); for men it is more a way of gaining some self-distance *within* the dominant culture.

The Birmingham men's group met once a week for two years (1973–5). During this time there was a fluctuating membership of a dozen or so, but there was a core of five. None of us had met before; and though we were all middle class, our 'middle classness' differed – ranging from the son of a clergyman, to the son of a garage proprietor. We were all in our twenties, and lived in different areas of Birmingham. Three had had a university education, and two were still students. One, after five years as a draughtsman, was on the 'dole'; one, who had left school at fifteen, was a production designer in a large engineering firm; and one was a bookshopkeeper. One (myself) was single, four were married, three were fathers with young children.

But none of us really knew what we wanted from a men's group. Domestic pressure, it seemed, had propelled us this far – together with unconscious dissatisfactions with our work, our relations with our parents, our masculine identities. Our personalities reflected the diversity of our backgrounds – some (noticeably the 'students') being openly assertive and articulate; others (the 'workers') remaining wary and unfathomable. How could we unscramble this mixture of experience?

Initial uncertainties were compounded by difficulties of communication. Perhaps everyone is reticent about talking about themselves. And though our meetings were held in people's homes, and were informal, there was an inevitable routine of introductions and building confidence. We began to discover that we had no language of feeling. We were trapped in public, specialized languages of work, learned in universities or factories, which acted as a shield against deeper emotional solidarities. When we talked about ourselves and our experiences, these would be presented through the public languages, in abstract, formal ways. The factory manager actually talked about himself as if he 'functioned', like a machine. The student-philosopher spoke about his 'bad faith', and his struggle to 'be authentic'. And the man on the dole, in this context, kept silent – and was perceived to be incoherent, swept along by a fluid, introspective experience.

Within the group we evolved a practice of 'self-deconstruction'. One person would speak about himself, his perspectives, in particular situations (work, family life, sexual relationships) and the others, at first, would just listen. Listening, without interrupting, was the first thing we had to learn to do. The experience of speaking, at length, to other men about your life, was itself disconcerting. You began to feel detached from your own 'persona'. There was an element of unintentional self-parody, and speakers would often have to re-think, or deny what they had said: 'Well, it wasn't quite like that'; or, 'Perhaps that's only partly true.' The self-detachment achieved through speaking began to give meaning to the notion of 'consciousness-raising'. For it became possible to say the unsayable, to open up closed areas of identity.

For the group as a whole, self-parody was a basis for mutual acceptance – beyond the role-playing, and the debating techniques, of traditional masculinity. Each individual was allowed to assume a formal identity ('academic', 'worker', 'drop-out') only in so far as he began to move beyond it. At times 'self-deconstruction' was directly encouraged, by ruthless questioning, and by focusing on the position of the individual within the group itself. Anything which had been overlooked, or seemed ambiguous, or simply did not 'ring true', was re-presented for the speaker's own clarification: 'What did you mean when you said x?'; 'I don't understand how x fits in with y,' etc. In this way, talking about your experience involved simultaneously questioning its apparent coherence, and reformulating it from a many-sided perspective.

Out of this process we began to develop an 'inter-personality' – an experience of which the focus was not a single individual, but the group itself. In part, this grew out of a structure of overlapping personal accounts. Each person's life contained some masculine experiences that were familiar to us all, and one of the most important sources of confidence was a look of recognition: 'Yes, I've felt that too'; 'I've had a similar experience.' Particularly important here were discussions of sexuality – as we recounted male fantasies of women, and feelings of sexual desire. It seemed that the splits in our heads – images of power and submissiveness – were expressive of ambivalent behaviour – moments of aggression and sensitivity. Was this a common masculine syndrome?

And through the technique of 'self-deconstruction', we began to discover each other's limitations. Listening to people's self-presentations involves building imaginary pictures of their lives – projecting yourself into their personal worlds. As we grew to know each other, the 'look of recognition' could be placed, not simply as a response to a person's 'character', but as an awareness of the contradictions of his identity. The questions we asked became leading questions – worrying away at repeated rationalizations, taking on a direction dictated by the individual himself. Not only did this allow an exploration of personal intuitions; it was also the foundation for a kind of group empathy – a mutual responsiveness.

For one of our preoccupations had to be the nature of the group itself: what it was doing as an entity, the different positions of group members, who was dominating (by defining the topics or asking the questions) and who was silent, who responded to whom, in what way. At times it was a kind of encounter group – as we talked about each other, touched each other, spent weekends together. The physical side of things – how we presented ourselves by sitting, dressing, gesturing – became as important as the verbal.

We had formed, in effect, a kind of peer-group. And as with any peer-group culture the intensity of individual involvement was rooted in an esoteric collective identity. This identity was amorphous, chaotic, and is impossible, in detail, to recall. Our conversations developed loosely, were easily side-tracked, involved hours of the most minute observations. What emerged from the group therefore, was not so much a 'theory of masculinity', as a rather vague, somewhat incoherent 'perspective'. None of us could really say why, but we were beginning to experience our immediate world in a fresh, exciting way. It was possible, by being silent oneself, and watchful, to begin to perceive the nuances of social interaction. At least this was a step beyond the blind self-confidence of traditional masculinity. It also seemed important, in a world dictated by career-schedules, to slow down, to make more flexible routines – cooking, cleaning, being with children. To some extent our group evolved a respect for inarticulacy; and encouraged the open expression of previously-tabooed feelings – what made us angry, what made us cry.

One 'theme' that did crystallize out of our men's group, was the recurring problem of couple relationships. For everyone, an immediate reason for his joining the group was the feminist challenge to male sexuality; and in part, the group acted as a therapeutic forum for a struggle encountered within sexual relationships. Our meetings were dominated by accounts of conflicts, jealousies, and reconciliations. In almost every respect our experience was ambivalent. We were in favour of women's independence, but felt threatened by it. We wanted to renounce our aggressive role, but felt bound to it. We were tired of disputes and petty squabbles, but had no power to stop them. Even though we were searching for a unified sexuality, we still felt impelled to 'perform' – and to watch ourselves performing. These emotional complexes seemed to us to be inherent within 'nuclear' relationships. The 'nuclear family' was a trap, both for women and for men, because it demanded *polarized* gender-roles: 'assertive'/'submissive'; 'decisive'/'uncertain'; 'detached'/ 'dependent'; etc. However 'complementary' these may seem to be, they are, at a deeper level, devisive – a potential source of friction.

One of the aspects of the group which I found particularly exciting was the way our 'perspective' had formed. For my education had given me an academic language deceptive in its apparent flexibility, with which I could seize on aspects of experience, but could not express their total, personal significance. In the group I was forced to learn the difference between analysis and abstraction – that it it not enough, for example, when discussing 'conscience', to talk blithely on about the 'super-ego'. Fears of making initiatives, of 'stepping out of line', are supported by intellectual rationalization, and lack of personal disclosure. I realized that the social theories I had learned applied to the society of which I was a part; that I was defined by the ideologies I criticized. So there was a continual attempt to find links between ideas and experiences – criticizing the ideas if they collapsed, or did not seem to fit, the complexities of experience.

But at a certain point in the group's development, the process of 'consciousness-raising' seemed to achieve a kind of 'resolution'. On one level, there remained a persistent problem of being unable to 'reconcile' different individual perspectives. Our masculine identities, though shared, were to some extent divergent – the products of varying kinds of work and family background. Against this variation, the collective dynamic of the group (and this may be a particular feature of men's groups, where 'chauvinist' tendencies are always present) itself became an analytic barrier. Individual accounts became predictable, the humour 'matey', the supportive atmosphere a little too cosy. At this point, which our group reached after about a year of meetings, 'consciousness-raising' faced a problem of further development. With the crystallization of a group 'perspective', the limits of inter-personality were reached.

In the Birmingham men's group (and we were by no means unique in this respect) this problem of further development was never fully articulated. We were faced with a complex question of self-definition, both of our social position as men, and of the political implications of our practice – which were not clearly recognized at the time. In retrospect, and in very general terms, I think two implicit considerations can be differentiated; for it is both necessary for us to comprehend the significance of 'consciousness-raising' as an activity (in part, we need a theory of consciousness, which defines the process of 'becoming conscious' – through individual awareness and interpersonal relationships – in terms which go beyond our immediate situation); and, second, because masculinity is social, rooted in the organization of work and family life, we are forced to recognize its practical implications. Without an attempt to change our lives, our critique of masculinity will remain one-sided.

The production of a theory of consciousness remains a

specialized task, beyond the scope of any particular group – and I can only attempt to outline some preliminary definitions. I think we need to understand more about the relationship between social experience and the structures which define that experience. The process of 'consciousness-raising' seems to support the Marxist theory[3] that within a social formation (which is ultimately determined by relations of production) there are two kinds of defining structure: not only social institutions (school, legal system, mass media, etc., constituting a 'State Apparatus'); but also 'general ideologies' (located in types of ritual, and language). Social consciousness is as much structured by the 'codes' of a general ideological discourse, as it is by institutional boundaries and rules of behaviour. Patriarchy is a 'general ideology' substantially carried by codes of speech ('Wait till your father gets home') and by inherited rituals and customs (like 'initiation ceremonies' at work). Through language, patriarchy remains a powerful source of definition, even when the primary institution in which it is located – the family – has lost many of its former functions to the capitalist state. The language of patriarchy is communicated, for the most part, unconsciously, in early childhood, before the individual learns ways of speaking associated with the 'State Apparatus' as such.

I can offer little more than a sketch. Part of the problem is that patriarchal ideology, which defines the experience of masculinity, is extraordinarily diverse and detailed. I think this is possibly because, as an unconscious language, patriarchy permeates all the 'official' definitions of state institutions. It is in this language that the power of men is enshrined. It is the social language of which 'man', as such, is the subject: an assertive language of politics and the market-place; a rational language which makes definitions and connections – the language of abstraction. It is also in the silences of this language that a repressed masculinity is imprisoned – as abstraction formalizes a man's identity, as rationality represses irrationality.

Becoming conscious of masculinity thus not only involves

[3] Readers familiar with his work will recognize the terminology of Louis Althusser. I have here adopted, somewhat eclectically, his thesis on 'Ideology and Ideological State Apparatuses', as developed in *Lenin and Philosophy and other Essays*.

transforming social institutions, but also understanding the language of patriarchy. And 'consciousness-raising' is, perhaps, an activity appropriate to linguistic transformation. It requires learning a new way of speaking, which needs to accompany the deconstruction of masculinity.

An emphasis on language, in the analysis of patriarchy, has been an important focus of the Women's Movement. A new appreciation of the 'politics of language' has perhaps been the substantial contribution of feminist theory (in the works of Sheila Rowbotham and Juliet Mitchell for example) to traditional definitions of class struggle. As Sheila Rowbotham puts it:

> 'The underground language of people who have no power to define and determine themselves in the world develops its own density and precision. It enables them to sniff the wind, sense the atmosphere, defend themselves in a hostile terrain. But it restricts them by affirming their own dependence upon the words of the powerful. It reflects their inability to break out of the imposed reality through to a reality they can define and control for themselves ... On the other hand the language of theory – removed language – only expresses a reality experienced by the oppressors. It speaks only for their world from their point of view. Ultimately a revolutionary movement has to break the hold of the dominant group over theory, it has to structure its own connections.'
>
> (Sheila Rowbotham, 1973b:32–3)

The Women's Liberation Movement has shown how becoming conscious of social contradictions involves a reappropriation of dominant languages, and a vocal liberation of their repressed silences.

But here, from the 'masculine' point of view, it is necessary to re-examine the 'reality experienced by the oppressors'. There is a sense in which feminist analysis sometimes tends to reduce the complexity of the 'dominant' world. Men do, of course, inherit patriarchal identities, and reproduce these identities in their own lives. The language of patriarchy thus perpetuates the oppression of women. As we have seen however, patriarchy operates by giving to men a family-based image of *work*, which is then reaffirmed by a work-based masculine culture. It is because of his status as a *worker*, that a man is able to possess, not only his wages, but also the language of buying and selling that dominates public life. And it is possession of this cultural power that provides him with some kind of explanation for the grind of alienated labour. It is thus crucial that, subjectively, such an explanation 'fits' his experience of working; and objectively, that his patriarchal aspirations are rewarded by the economic mode of production.

In these ways, the experience of consciousness-raising points towards a complex analysis of the operations of ideology. And it is necessary to understand how 'becoming conscious' of these operations provides a basis for their subsequent transformation. Ideology possesses concrete significance because it defines social consciousness; and if the ideological mechanism is itself a focus of struggle, it must be adequately theoretically described. Ideology can neither be represented in abstraction, as 'above' social determinations; nor can it be reduced to the passive 'reflection' of material life. One task of social theory is to comprehend the *dialectics* of meaning – partly pre-given and partly created – through which 'general ideologies' are constituted.

This understanding of patriarchy, as an ideological imposition, implies a further set of practical, and 'political' questions. For if the experience of masculinity is socially prestructured, how can it be changed? What is the defining power of patriarchy in the routines of daily existence? Again, in the Birmingham men's group, our answers to these questions remained far from satisfactory. A common interest in 'sexual politics' seemed to provide a starting-point – and we attempted, by analogy with the Women's Movement, to construct for ourselves a combination of 'personal' and 'political' projects. At the local level we helped in a preschool play-group run by Women's Liberation,[4] and made some, individual gestures towards restructuring sex-

[4] For a summary, and critical account of the Birmingham Women's Liberation Playgroup, including extensive discussion of problems of men and childcare, see: *Out of the Pumpkin Shell*, a pamphlet published by Birmingham Women's Liberation ('further reading').

roles. Nationally, we participated in 'Men Against Sexism' – a bi-annual conference of men's groups, which published a newsletter, and developed a national network. From 1973–5 there were about forty such groups in various cities throughout the country.[5]

But in all our practical activities, we faced an immediate contradiction. As men, as the agents of a patriarchal culture, we remained the dominant gender. In a certain sense, we were imperialists in a rebellion of slaves – concerned, defensively, about the threat to our privilege. The very notion of 'men's politics' was paradoxical. We had no experience of sexual oppression, violence, jokes at our expense. There were no issues to unite us – no basis for action against a system that already operates in our favour. This paradox was driven home by gay men at Men Against Sexism conferences. Above all, we had not 'come out' – we remained heterosexual, embarrassed at being thought gay, typical liberal men.

In the confusion of our position, these charges touched a core. We hoped to contribute to sexual politics – but were, apparently by definition, disqualified. The political contradiction was reflected in practical uncertainty, as we remained disabled by our masculinity. We tried to publicize ourselves – by speaking at meetings and to the local press – but failed to produce a consistent self-definition. We continued to explore personal projects – collective childcare, a 'denucleated' family life-style – but these remained within a 'progressive' middle-class culture. It would perhaps be wrong to entirely underestimate these activities: some did crystallize as 'alternative' institutions – the play-group, a food co-op, a radical press. With the support of the group some individuals succeeded in changing jobs, living in collective houses, achieving some independence from the family. But all these remained personal, or at least local, solutions to general social questions. And always, as 'straight men' we were wary and peripheral, in relation to their outcome.

[5] For readers who are specifically interested in the phenomenon of men's groups in Britain, I have included a selective guide to 'men's literature', including newsletters and articles on 'Men Against Sexism', in 'further reading'.

Moreover, it is crucial, both for our tentative development and our subsequent demise, that we failed to confront our political position. For even though we did recognize, intuitively, the truth of the gay accusation – we preferred to avoid its implications. We continued to interpret our personalized practices through the politics of feminism. We continued to speak of 'men's liberation'; and to assume that we could parallel, even complement, the activities of Women's Liberation. By this token we internalized the masculine paradox – defining ourselves in terms of sexual oppression, as the guilty, oppressive agency – but we avoided the logical outcome. We held on, wishfully, to a kind of negative ideal, a self-destructive utopia.

As long as we adopted this contradictory definition, our confusion was inevitable. In the first place, we could not comprehend the transition from the small group to a wider political basis. Consciousness-raising remains a vitally necessary experience – but practical solutions to the problems it poses cannot be 'experientially' found. As it has been the purpose of this book to show, the experience of individual men is constituted by a whole social system of work and domestic life. And the transformation of this system, including its 'gender-roles', must remain a collective responsibility.

Equally however, and perhaps more significantly, we failed to appreciate the limits of masculinity itself. This is a difficult observation, but one I want finally to make – because I think straight men must recognize, openly, the truth of the gay and feminist position. Not only are different gender-identities ('feminine', 'gay', 'masculine') distinctively irreducible; they also fundamentally contradict, and do not simply 'complement' each other. The relation between the sexes cannot be 'symmetrical': it is incongruent – and, as men have had to learn, is constructed in terms of social *power* ('oppression'). To simply deny, or vaguely wish to 'relinquish', the reality of this power is to fall victim to a liberal myopia. And to assume that men can, unproblematically, experience 'men's liberation' – that there are any analogies with gay or feminist politics – is, in the end, an illusion. It is perhaps understandable that in the first, exciting years of the new feminism 'progressive' men should have shared this illusion. But men's 'consciousness' is not women's consciousness – and men's 'consciousness-raising' shows the impossibility of a 'men's politics'.

To reach this conclusion is not however, simply 'negative'. Discovering the political limits of masculinity is not a recipe for inactivity. Men can, I think, with a limited sphere, develop a supportive role which does not 'incorporate' feminist and gay initiatives. It is important that men should continue to participate in childcare and nursery education (creches, playgroups, etc.) where their very presence challenges sex-role expectations. Some men may involve themselves in 'community' action – working with tenants' organizations, squatting, building play-centres, and free schools – which often co-exists with explict feminist activities. Often, it seems, the most successful men's groups have been related to neighbourhood centres or newspapers – where sexual politics is part of an involvement in local political work.

And in particular, men who are convinced of the importance of sexual politics must, I think, begin to find ways of articulating their position. For socialist men especially, it is necessary to challenge a prevailing left-wing sectarianism which relegates questions of personal and family life to peripheral status – as 'women's issues'. Feminists and gays have themselves criticized the chauvinism of the left – its dogmatic formulas, its predictable 'party-lines'. Both groups have initiated a far-reaching debate with a male-dominated socialist tradition. It is vital that 'men against sexism' begin to take a constructive position within this debate – supporting the attention to personal experience, and the critique of socialist dogmatism, which sections of the Women's Movement have especially pioneered.[6]

I hope that this book has contributed to that possibility. I have tried to establish that masculinity, and men's personal experiences, are necessarily socially constructed. And I have argued that a man's gender-identity is interwoven with the ideology of 'free-individuality' which supports the system of

[6] Again, the classic texts are those of Sheila Rowbotham and Juliet Mitchell (see 'further reading'). The key periodicals are: for socialist feminism, *Red Rag* (22, Murray Mews, London W1); and for the relationship between gay liberation and socialism, *Gay Left* (c/o 36a, Craven Road, London W2).

capitalist wage-labour. If, as with Tom, the pressures of work become too great; or, as with Bill, a man faces the threat of redundancy – the reversal is both socio-economic and personal. In personal terms, the loss of social power is experienced as a crisis of gender-identity. If it is true that the 'solutions' to personal problems cannot themselves be 'personal' (for they symptomatically point to a complex social structure) – it is not, by the same token, simply 'idealist', or 'diversionary' to recognize the personal level. The challenge to socialist men is to understand masculinity as a social problem – and thus to work together for a non-sexist socialist society.

References

ALTHUSSER, LOUIS (1971) *Lenin and Philosophy and Other Essays*. London: New Left Books.

ARENSBERG, C. M. and KIMBALL, S. T. (1968) *Family and Community in Ireland* (2nd edition). Cambridge, Mass.: Harvard U.P.

BENGIS, INGRID (1973) *Combat In The Erogenous Zone*. London: Wildwood House.

BERGER, JOHN (1972a) *Ways of Seeing*. Harmondsworth: Penguin.

—— (1972b) *G*. London: Weidenfeld and Nicolson.

BERGER, JOHN and MOHR, JEAN (1975) *A Seventh Man*. Harmondsworth: Penguin.

BEYNON, HUW (1973) *Working For Ford*. Harmondsworth: Penguin.

BLYTHE, RONALD (1969) *Akenfield*. London: Allen Lane.

BROWN, RICHARD, BRANNEN, PETER, COUSINS, JIM, and SAMPHIER, MICHAEL (1973) Leisure in Work: The 'Occupational Culture' of Shipbuilding workers. In M. Smith, S. Parker, C. Smith (eds), *Leisure and Society in Britain*. London: Allen Lane.

BURNETT, JOHN (ed.) (1974) *Useful Toil*. London: Allen Lane.

KITSON CLARK, G. (1962) *The Making of Victorian England*. London: Methuen.

COMER, LEE (1974) *Wedlocked Women*. Leeds: Feminist Press.

GOLDTHORPE, JOHN, LOCKWOOD, DAVID, BECHHOFER, F., and PLATT, J. (1968) *The Affluent Worker: Industrial Attitudes and Behaviour*. Cambridge: Cambridge University Press.

HARTLEY, RUTH E. (1974) Sex-Role Pressures and the Socialization of the Male Child. In Joseph Pleck and Jack Sawyer (eds), *Men and Masculinity*. Englewood Cliffs, N.J.: Prentice-Hall.

LAING, R. D. (1960) *The Divided Self*. London: Tavistock.

LAWRENCE, D. H. (1954) *Women In Love* (new edition). London: Heinemann.

LESSING, DORIS (1965) *A Proper Marriage*. London: MacGibbon and Kee.

MARSDEN, DENNIS (1968) In the Mill. In Brian Jackson (ed.), *Working Class Community*. London: Routledge & Kegan Paul.

MARSDEN, DENNIS and DUFF, EUAN (1975) *Workless*. Harmondsworth: Penguin.

MARX, KARL (1970) *1844 Manuscripts* (ed. Dirk J. Struik). London: Lawrence and Wishart.

MILES, JOHN (1973) Jealousy. *Spare Rib* (September).

MOYNIHAN, MICHAEL (ed.) (1975) *A Place Called Armageddon. Letters from the Great War*. London: David & Charles.

OAKLEY, ANN (1972) *Sex, Gender and Society*. Melbourne: Temple Smith.

RAVEN, SUSAN (1973) Anyone for Open Marriage? *The Sunday Times*, January 28.

REICH, WILHELM (1972) *The Mass Psychology of Fascism*. London: Souvenir Press.

ROWBOTHAM, SHEILA (1973a) *Hidden from History*. London: Pluto Press.

——(1973b) *Woman's Consciousness, Man's World*. Harmondsworth: Penguin.

SANDISON, ALAN (1967) *The Wheel of Empire*. London: Macmillan.

SAWYER, JACK (1974) On Male Liberation. In Pleck and Sawyer (eds), *Men and Masculinity*.

SEABROOK, JEREMY (1971) *City Close Up*. London: Allen Lane.

SIGAL, CLANCY (1969) 144 Piccadilly. *New Society*, October 9.

WILLIAMS, RAYMOND (1958) *Culture and Society*. London: Chatto and Windus.

Woodhouse Grove School, Old Grovian Assoc., Apperley Bridge, Bradford, Yorks (1962) *Woodhouse Grove School 1812–1962*.

YOUNG, MICHAEL and WILLMOTT, PETER (1962) *Family and Kinship in East London*. Harmondsworth: Penguin.

—— (1973) *The Symmetrical Family*. London: Routledge & Kegan Paul.

ZARETSKY, ELI (1976) *Capitalism, The Family and Personal Life*. London: Pluto Press.

Suggestions for further reading

As a stimulus to further critical work on masculinity I would like to suggest the following reading:

(1) Undoubtedly the two feminist books which have had most impact and direct relevance for men are: Ingrid Bengis, *Combat in the Erogenous Zone*; and Sheila Rowbotham, *Woman's Consciousness, Man's World* (see references above). The latter is an especially formative attempt to relate questions of consciousness and experience to issues of politics and theory, and should be read in conjunction with two classic statements of feminist politics: Sheila Rowbotham's 'Women's Liberation and the New Politics', in *The Body Politic*, Writings from the Women's Liberation Movement in Britain 1969–72, compiled by Michelene Wandor (London: Stage 1 Press, 1972); and Juliet Mitchell's *Women's Estate* (Harmondsworth: Penguin, 1971). Problems of political organization within the Women's Movement (consciousness-raising, informal small-groups) are critically focused in the pamphlet, *The Tyranny of Structurelessness*, by Jo Free-

man (reprinted by the Anarchist Workers Association, 13, Coltman Street, Hull). A stimulating contribution to the theory and practice of sexual politics has been made by Red Collective, a London-based mixed group (104, Greencroft Gardens, London NW6) whose two pamphlets, *The Politics of Sexuality in Capitalism*, I & II, contain an important critique of the family.

(2) Underlying the growth of 'consciousness-raising' is the complex 'counter-cultural' radicalism of the 'sixties, and readers who are especially interested in its development should consult: Peter Stansill and David Zane Mairowitz (eds), *Bamn, Outlaw Manifestos and Ephemera 1965–70* (Harmondsworth: Penguin, 1971); and Christopher Gray (ed.) *Leaving the 20th Century, The Incomplete Work of the Situationist International* (Free Fall Publications, 1974). An introduction to subjective and interpersonal aspects of this experience is provided by the work of R. D. Laing, especially *Knots* (London: Tavistock Publications, 1970); and *The Politics of Experience* (Harmondsworth: Penguin, 1967). Aspects of radical psycho-therapy, encounters, etc., are examined in reprints of *Issues in Radical Therapy* (IRT Collective, P.O. Box 23544, Oakland, Calif. 94623) – nos. 2, 'Radical Therapy and Revolution'; 3, 'Letter to a Brother'; 8, 'Between Men and Women'; and 10, 'Fighting Men's Oppression', being particularly relevant to the critique of masculinity.

In this context a resurgence of political interest in psychoanalysis, especially the works of Wilhelm Reich (see, *The Sexual Revolution*, Vision Press paperback, 1972, and *What Is Class Consciousness?*, and other political writings of Reich, from Socialist Reproduction, 57d, Jamestown Road, London NW1) underpins two important pamphlets of the early 'seventies: *The Irrational in Politics*, by Maurice Brinton (Solidarity Pamphlet No. 33, c/o 123, Lathom Road, London E6); and *You As A Product* (Red Ink Publications, Newcastle University Socialist Society).

(3) Literature on masculinity itself tends to be haphazard and difficult to find. Two highly recommended American introductions are: Joseph Pleck and Jack Sawyer (eds) *Men and Masculinity* (see reference above), a collection of articles on Men's Liberation/Men Against Sexism; and *Unbecoming Men, A Men's*

Consciousness-Raising Group writes on Oppression and Themselves (New York: Times Change Press, 1971). Back issues (four) of the British Men Against Sexism newsletter, variously titled *Brothers*, *Men Against Sexism*, *Brothers Against Sexism*, can be obtained (photocopies) from Rising Free, 142, Drummond Street, London W1. For the development of men's groups in Britain consult: Ian Jones, 'An Introduction to Men Against Sexism', *Peace News*, September 20, 1974; Paul Harrison, 'Burn Your Jock Straps', *New Society*, May 15, 1975 (not as banal as its title suggests); and Keith Paton, 'there comes a time when the only anger is love', *Peace News*, April 3, 1976 (a provocative, explicitly utopian, discussion of possibilities for men's politics). The most eloquent piece to emerge from the 'men's movement' in Britain is John Miles' 'Jealousy', *Spare Rib*, September 1973.

Other relevant pamphlets/articles on men and childcare include: *The Children's Community Centre* (No. 2) (123, Dartmouth Park Hill, London N19); and *Out of the Pumpkin Shell, Running a Women's Liberation Playgroup* (Birmingham, 1975), (available from Feminist Books, P.O. Box HP5, Leeds LS6 1LN). Extracts from the latter, and a review, are reprinted in 'Including Fathers: Men talk about Playgroup', *Contact Magazine*, March 1976.

Finally, for a stimulating theoretical discussion of patriarchal ideology and male domination see Eli Zaretsky, 'Male Supremacy and the Unconscious', in *Socialist Revolution*, Vol. 4, Nos. 3–4 (January 1975).

Index

affluent society
   and progressive middle class,
      111–12, 115
   and working class, 67–8
aggression, and working-class re-
      lationships, 43, 45, 72
Akenfield, 53
alternative society, 10, 130
   institutions of, 143
Althusser, L., 140f
ambivalence, in masculine iden-
      tity, 24, 30, 48, 50
'anti-hero' cult, 113, 114
Arensberg, C. M., 52
authority in the home, 23, 32, 70,
      95
   removal of, 119

Bengis, Ingrid, 16–17, 18, 150

Berger, John, 7, 8, 38, 57
Beynon, Huw, 62, 63, 64–5
Blythe, Ronald, 53
boyhood
   culture of, 32
   development of masculinity in,
      23
   freedom and, 41
British Leyland, 72, 76–7
Brothers, Men's Liberation news-
      letter, 118f
Brown, Richard, 60
Burnett, John, 54, 55

capital, in middle-class work, 83
   'cultural', 83
capitalist societies
   masculinity and, 12, 14, 57–8
   structure of work in, 49

157